T0314954

Praise for the first edition of *The Strategic Leader's Roadmap*

"Thinking strategically and acting decisively are vital capabilities for running any enterprise, and the Wharton School's Harbir Singh and Michael Useem show how to develop and apply them together. *The Strategic Leader's Roadmap* offers an invaluable model for the strategic leadership required at all levels in any organization during the turbulent era ahead."

—Ajay Banga, Executive Chairman, MasterCard Inc.

"*The Strategic Leader's Roadmap* provides an essential playbook for combining business strategy with great leadership. In an era of heightened change and uncertainty, the exercise of both has become essential, and Harbir Singh and Michael Useem offer managers and executives compelling illustrations and practical guidance for doing so."

—William P. Lauder, Executive Chairman,
The Estée Lauder Companies Inc.

"For pragmatic direction on how best to combine a company's strategy and its leadership, *The Strategic Leader's Roadmap* is essential reading. Harbir Singh and Michael Useem have brought executive experience together with university research to identify *the* essential steps for the art of leading strategically."

—Maggie Wilderotter, former Chairman and CEO, Frontier
Communications; director, Costco, DreamWorks Animation,
Hewlett Packard Enterprise, and Juno Therapeutics

HARBIR SINGH AND MICHAEL USEEM

THE STRATEGIC LEADER'S ROADMAP

REVISED AND UPDATED EDITION

6 STEPS FOR INTEGRATING LEADERSHIP AND STRATEGY

WHARTON SCHOOL PRESS

Philadelphia

Published by Wharton School Press
The Wharton School
University of Pennsylvania
3620 Locust Walk
300 Steinberg Hall-Dietrich Hall
Philadelphia, PA 19104
Email: whartonschoolpress@wharton.upenn.edu
Website: wsp.wharton.upenn.edu/

Ebook ISBN: 978-1-61363-120-1
Paperback ISBN: 978-1-61363-121-8
Hardcover ISBN: 978-1-61363-152-2

Contents

Conclusion: Becoming a Strategic Leader 93

Introduction
Strategic Leadership as the Driver of Growth and Renewal

One of those light bulb moments happened when Apple cofounder Steve Jobs visited a Xerox lab in Silicon Valley in 1979. He learned of an experimental mouse and cursor for scrolling and clicking through menus and icons on a computer display. Xerox never commercialized the mouse and cursor, but Jobs's glance was enough for him to instantly appreciate the devices' enormous potential for navigating computer interfaces.

When Apple introduced Lisa in 1983, the first personal computer equipped with a cursor and mouse, the *New York Times* explained with wonder what would soon become commonplace for us all: "The mouse moves," and "the cursor—the arrow that points to particular places on the screen—moves accordingly." A year later, Apple added its mover and pointer to its new personal computer, the Macintosh, helping it become a runaway success, canonizing the interface devices, and launching the company on its way to the stratosphere. Apple's market value touched $2 trillion in 2020, the first US company to do so.[1]

Garrett Camp had experienced his own flash of insight when wondering how to reduce the cost of using black-car services, taxis dispatched rather than hailed on the street. After he and his friends had spent hundreds of dollars on rides, it dawned on him that they might cut their costs if they could somehow share the car services with others. Camp and Travis Kalanick created the ride-sharing company Uber to do just that, combining the smartphone, geolocation, and network communication. Kalanick took the helm of Uber in 2010 and soon transformed the fledgling start-up into a global behemoth.

While Steve Jobs and successor Tim Cook successfully converted Jobs's insights into America's most valued enterprise, Kalanick's leadership of Uber by contrast proved toxic. Uber's directors forced Kalanick out in 2017, believing their burgeoning business required far better hands on the tiller if its groundbreaking strategy was actually to generate growth.[2]

If a sailing ship without a qualified skipper is sure to flounder, it seems likely that a promising business model without a competent chief would suffer the same fate. And that is the thrust of what we advocate here: Good strategy *and* good leadership are equally essential for building a firm. They are two sides of the company coin, each different but both completely dependent on the other, the yin and yang of the enterprise.

Consider the strategy *and* leadership of Tricia Griffith, who joined the Progressive Corporation, a provider of auto and property insurance for millions, fresh out of college. She started in Indianapolis as a claims-representative trainee for auto damage, rotated up the ranks through a host of other functions, and reached the corner office in 2016.[3]

Griffith espoused a strategy of fast expansion, and under her leadership the company grew more than 20% annually, adding 8,400 new employees in 2019 alone. Progressive's net new premiums had jumped by 50% during her first three years as chief executive, pushing it to overtake Allstate as America's third-largest auto insurer after State Farm and Geico, and catapulting it onto the Fortune 100. *Fortune* magazine named Griffith "Businessperson of the Year" in 2020, and its headline for the best among the Fortune 500 asked readers to "meet the CEO of the insurance company growing faster than Apple."[4]

While Griffith had locked onto a strategy of aggressive growth, her personal style brought that strategy to life through a deft combination of presence, inclusion, and direction that let her personally energize but also focus the front lines. She described herself as being "out and about" as much as possible, and she pressed direct reports to do the same. The head of a company of 40,000 people, she nonetheless stopped to greet and swap the latest with just about everybody she encountered, some at their desks and others in the hallways. "I never take the elevator," she noted.

During one event to welcome new employees in 2019, a woman recruited from an archrival told how in the twelve years at her previous employer she had never met her boss's boss, let alone the chief executive. On meeting Griffith now, the newcomer was initially intimidated, but the CEO soon had her talking. "People feel like I'm the girl next door," Griffith explained.

Rather than boldly striding to the front of the welcome event as a deferential hush descended on the hundreds waiting to see "the big boss," Griffith worked the room, shaking hands and greeting everyone along her path, brushing past no one. And then, without a stage, riser, or lectern, she began speaking, appearing both personal and professional.

Griffith began her welcome with reference to her own college, Illinois State University, located coincidentally in the same town as archrival State Farm Insurance. The school was not the Ivy League, but it was solid—*U.S. News & World Report* ranked ISU 197th among 399 national universities in 2019—and that was partly her point. Like so many in the room, Griffith had credentials that reflected Middle America, and she stood with the newcomers, not above them. Her first job at Progressive, crawling under damaged cars and talking with injured customers, was hardly a fast-track entry point. The company itself was such an unknown quantity that when Griffith told her mother she was joining Progressive, her mother asked, "Oh, the soup company?"

Griffith added that she was forklift certified, a curious but instructive factoid. Her blue-collar working days were still part of her persona, which was also true for many in the room.

For Griffith, though, being a "people person" was not just a matter of personal presentation; it was how she sought to run the entire enterprise. Since insurance policies are so intangible, she explained, customers look especially to employee behavior as an embodiment of the company's character; and in her own experience, a degree of humility with a take-charge attitude were a pair of qualities she much valued.

Doing well by customers, Griffith found, brought them back again and again, a source of pride through her many years at the company. And now she viewed that same personal engagement by each new employee as essential for the company's future growth, an attitude she would have to generate. Employees were more likely to "bring their whole selves to work," she explained, if they had seen her whole self at work. When followers know something personal and appealing about the leader, they are more ready to stay the course. But that leadership presence had to be projected. "I'm a greeter," she said, with a disciplined gregariousness dating back to her six years as chief human resources officer, when she had learned to chat and relax with others, whatever their stature in the company.

Now as chief executive, Griffith ate in the employee lunch room on Fridays, where she often asked a table of employees if she could join them. Though some may have felt intimidated or "put on the spot," soon they were all talking animatedly about their plans for the weekend. Text messages flew: "I'm having lunch with the CEO!"

Projecting herself and her inclusiveness, however, was just the first half of Griffith's newcomer agenda. The other half was conveying the company's strategy to the new arrivals in ways they would personally embrace and never forget. Though always inclusive, she was equally directive. The company needed the fresh hires, she explained, and there was plenty of room for growth at Progressive, driven by new financial technologies and disruptive opportunities. And she wanted to sustain that growth to help Progressive become American consumers' first choice for auto insurance, one day overtaking State Farm and Geico. It would only be achievable, however, if the newcomers were drawn to both the business strategy and her leadership of it.

Strategic Leadership as the Driver of Company Growth and Renewal

We believe strategic leadership, the integrated application of both strategy and leadership, has become more important than ever—and is all the more vital for managers to master. This conviction has emerged from our research and observations of executives and companies. We have seen five trends emerge, placing an ever-greater value on the exercise of strategic leadership at the top and increasingly throughout the company ranks:

1. Companies are more globally interdependent and competitive, and shortcomings in either their strategy or their leadership are likely to have greater downside consequences than in a less connected world.[5]
2. The contracting life cycles for products and expanding change rates for markets have placed a greater premium on having a competitive strategy *and* an executive team in place that can execute it in timely fashion.
3. Firms are increasingly contending with not just direct competitors but also disruptive innovators and changeable customers. This has placed a greater premium on more vigilant company leaders and led to a greater readiness to adjust or even redirect strategies.
4. New markets in developing economies and growing markets at the bottom of the pyramid in advanced economies are attracting fast-acting and frugal competitors, and the agile exercise of strategic leadership has become critical for reaching and prospering in those leaner and faster-moving markets.[6]
5. Investors are placing greater pressure on company executives and directors to exercise more active strategic leadership of their enterprise.

We define the act of leading strategically as mastering the elements of strategy and leadership both separately and as an integrated whole. It requires applying them together and continually drawing on both as markets morph, disruptions occur, and openings arise. In framing strategy and leadership as a single unified discipline, we are seeking to see both components applied consistently and completely. Just one or the other will not suffice. Moreover, we believe strategic leadership is an acquired capability that can be mastered by managers at all levels in all companies. To that end, we suggest a roadmap for its strengthening, summarized in box I.1.

Each element of this list is vital. Mastery of one or even several elements will not accomplish much, but taken together these six items can serve as a roadmap for developing and applying strategic leadership. Becoming a more strategic leader is a tall order, but we

---

Box I.1. The Strategic Leader's Roadmap

1. **Integrate strategy and leadership.** Master the elements of strategy and leadership both separately and as an integrated whole.

2. **Learn to lead strategically.** Pursue directed learning, one-on-one coaching, and instructive experience to develop an integrated understanding of strategy and leadership.

3. **Ensure strategic fit.** Arrange a strong match between the strategic challenges of a managerial position and the individual with the leadership skills to fill it.

4. **Convey strategic intent.** Communicate strategic intent throughout the organization and empower others to implement the strategy.

5. **Layer leadership.** Ensure leaders at every level are capable of appreciating strategic intent and implementing it, and hold them responsible for its execution.

6. **Decide deliberatively.** Focus on both short- and long-term objectives, press for disciplined analysis and avoid status-quo bias, and bring the future into the present.

---

believe concentrating on personal development in all of these arenas will offer a more complete and more commanding way forward.

Why We Wrote This Book

The Strategic Leader's Roadmap builds on our personal experience working with students who aspire to manage and those who are already managing in a range of enterprises. As Wharton School management professors, we have had the opportunity to teach MBA students, executive MBA students, and midcareer managers in programs in the United States and globally. We have learned from them and from their employers that their present and future responsibilities increasingly require thinking strategically *and* leading effectively.

In an earlier era, a firm's chief strategist might not have had to ponder much about how to implement strategy. Or someone who led a start-up might not have had to give much thought to its long-term growth. That segmentation is no longer acceptable. The jobs desired by many students and managers increasingly require both. As a result, in our MBA program we combine elements of strategy and leadership in management courses, viewing them as mutually reinforcing facets of a single skill set. Similarly, in our midcareer initiatives, we bring strategy into our leadership programs and leadership into our strategy programs. And we see both well combined in the managers at many companies we work with.

Since we have also found that strategic leadership knows no geographical boundaries, we draw on our academic research, organizational consulting, and personal contact with companies and managers across markets not only in North America but also in Africa, Asia, Europe, and Latin America.

In part I, we delve into the main principles of strategy and leadership. In part II, we elaborate on the roadmap by developing each of its six main components.

In part III, we see what strategic leadership looks like in several companies where it has proved important for enterprise growth and shareholder value. We take you into the offices—and the mindsets—of those who have been called to think and act strategically, including John Chambers, chief executive officer of Cisco Systems; Lawrence Culp, CEO of Danaher Corporation; A. G. Lafley, CEO of Procter & Gamble Co.; Jack Ma, founder and executive chairman of Alibaba Group; Indra Nooyi, chief executive of PepsiCo; and Denise Ramos, CEO of ITT Inc. And we profile other companies where strategic leadership has also proved important, including the United States' Apple Inc., Britain's GlaxoSmithKline PLC, and China's Lenovo Group Ltd.

By witnessing what successful strategic leaders have done and asking how they learned to do so, we will all be better prepared to learn and apply the main principles to our own thoughts and actions. As business historian Richard S. Tedlow observed, Intel Corporation's legendary chief executive Andrew "Andy" Grove was "America's greatest student and teacher of business. By analyzing the decisions he made on the road to becoming a great leader, you can learn to hone your own leadership skills." As a direct extension of that premise, by watching others exercise their strategic leadership skills—or sometimes fall short—we can learn to better exercise our own skill set.[7]

Finally, in part IV, we take you into the boardrooms and the institutions that preside over and invest in the strategic leaders we have chronicled here. With the concentration of shareholding in the hands of a relatively small number of professional investors, both directors and investors have come to insist that their boards be more engaged in the company strategy and more vigilant in selecting executives who can lead the company. Here we follow China's Lenovo Group as it restructured its board to play a stronger role in leading the company's acquisition of IBM's personal computer division and in expanding abroad, and we look at activist investors in the United States as they have pressed companies like Yahoo Inc. to bring in more talented and more strategic top management teams.

First, let's begin with the fundamentals of strategy and leadership that all executives, directors, and investors will want to incorporate into their thinking and their actions.

PART I

Strategy and Leadership Fundamentals

Chapter 1

Principles of Strategy and Leadership

IKEA, the Swedish-based home furnishing company with more than 375 stores in 30 countries and annual revenue of more than $45 billion in 2019, has a simple vision statement.

"Our mission as a business is 'to offer a wide range of well-designed, functional home furnishing products at prices so low that as many people as possible will be able to afford them.' Our vision also goes beyond home furnishing. We want to create a better everyday for all people impacted by our business."[1]

The company's strategy is to offer exceptionally low prices that other providers cannot match or sustain, making IKEA's products more affordable to more customers. At the same time, the company promises a smaller sacrifice in the aesthetics of its less costly products, stressing that the products will be well designed and the company will not be stigmatized as a cut-rate brand. And in creating "a better everyday life for the many people," IKEA included its own employees, not just customers, by paying workers above-market wages.[2]

A first step toward integrating strategy and leadership is to understand the basic dynamics of an organization's current strategy. This necessitates applying an active ear to the market and having the ability to translate disparate sources, weak signals, and nascent trends into a vision of where to take an enterprise. And this must be done recurrently, since no single moment of insight can serve as an enduring platform. It requires an ability to read the past's implications for future decisions and to learn from prior experiences which actions will better serve the enterprise in the future. It also depends on a manager's capacity to communicate that intent persuasively and indelibly.[3]

Company strategy can be defined as setting the firm's general direction and identifying what creates sustainable value and advantage for the firm. Underpinning the strategy is a broader *vision* with aspirational goals, providing both an overarching trajectory for the firm and an inspiration for employees to achieve it.

Setting company strategy, in the way IKEA has, requires leaders to devote time and thought to five sets of questions, summarized in box 1.1.

Vision and Competitive Positioning

A company's vision shapes the competitive positioning of its products and services. To enact the vision, managers require an appreciation for the drivers of both differentiation and cost to define and sustain that positioning. This can be challenging since industries vary greatly in the degree of product differentiation and cost, which affects customer willingness to pay.

IKEA managers, for instance, achieved a sophisticated combination of differentiation and cost by offering simple, versatile products with smart designs at a very low price point. By focusing on clean lines in furniture design and easy-to-assemble kits, its managers were able to provide customers with aesthetically pleasing products at an attractive price and, in doing so, build an enduring competitive position in the home furnishing market.

Or consider the competitive positioning and product differentiation of Procter & Gamble Co. (P&G), a consumer goods firm with $75 billion in revenue in 2020 and more than 99,000 employees. Former chief executive A. G. Lafley, who led the company from 2000 to 2010 and again from 2013 to 2015, set forward the firm's vision: "We will provide products and services of superior quality and value that improve the lives of the world's consumers. As a result, consumers will reward us with leadership sales, profit, and

Box 1.1. Setting Company Strategy

1. **Vision.** Do you have an inspirational statement of purpose and direction for the organization? What is your winning aspiration? How does this drive your organization's goals, sense of purpose, and approach to competition and achievement of ambition?

2. **Competitive positioning.** How is the firm positioned in its markets? The time-proven concepts of competitive strategy are of primary concern, including the influence of suppliers, the likelihood of new entrants, the threat of substitutes, and the firm's position in its collaborative networks.

3. **Value proposition.** What features of a company's product or service line create value—or destroy value—and are subject to a manager's discretion? What investments are needed to enhance product or service differentiation or improve efficiency?

4. **Competitive advantage.** Given the external and internal factors, what decisions by a manager can create additional advantage for the enterprise in the market? Expressed negatively, what bad decisions or cases of indecision can result in disadvantage?

5. **Strategic redirection.** In light of answers to the previous questions, is the enterprise due for a course correction?

---

value creation, allowing our people, our shareholders, and the communities we live and work in, to prosper."[4]

While the statement may appear lofty or even contrived, it served as a pragmatic vision for focusing Lafley and employees on developing products that could "improve the lives" of consumers, though consumers might pay more for them. The number of well-known billion-dollar P&G brands that achieved this—Crest, Duracell, Gillette, Olay, Pampers, and Tide among them—more than doubled during Lafley's tenure at P&G, and he built a fivefold increase in the number of less established brands with sales of $500 million to $1 billion.[5]

Some industries, such as fashion, pharmaceuticals, and smart-phones, present opportunities for high product differentiation, whereas other industries have less of an opportunity. When product differentiation is low, companies tend to focus on greater efficiency and lower costs compared with competitors. One example: the discount retail industry, where a primary driver of a firm's competitive advantage is its low prices, made possible by intensive effort within the firm to cut costs as much as possible. Walmart has long dominated this industry with its exceptionally low expenses in its supply chain, using real-time inventory and logistic systems to reduce stockpile costs and the expense of selling in its stores. Its managers deliberately set forward a long-term, low-cost model built on a superior supply chain and global manufacturing system. Other players in the online retail market have optimized a combination of differentiation and efficiency, delivering products exceptionally quickly and inexpensively.

In industries with greater potential for product differentiation, brand can prove a potent driver. Customers are willing to pay more for beverages made by the Coca-Cola Company and PepsiCo, for example, than for those made by lesser-known companies, even when taste tests reveal little real disparity among them. Similarly, customers are prepared to spend more on fragrances from the Estée Lauder Companies and L'Oréal S.A. than those from less prestigious makers, and clients are willing to spend more on consulting firms with premier reputations, such as McKinsey & Company, and well-known investment banks, such as Goldman Sachs.

Technology has become a differentiator as well. Lipitor, the cholesterol-reducing drug produced by Pfizer, earned more than $1.97 billion in revenue in 2019. Many physicians and patients continue to prefer Pfizer's offering not only because its prescriptions do not require a special liver test but also because they are already familiar with the brand. Customer service is yet another example of a differentiator, as evident among exclusive hotels and luxury stores that charge customers a premium for their high-class ambiance.[6]

Most firms start with relatively similar inputs to create their products, but efficiencies in making them can vary considerably. From purchasing and manufacturing to marketing and distribution, reducing costs can help move a company toward a *superior value frontier* where the combination of product differentiation and production cost is optimal given the enterprise and its market. For optimizing their competitive positioning, managers are called to focus on four features of their firm's strategy, as outlined in box 1.2.

A *superior value proposition* is the combination of differentiated product features and costs that most appeals to customers. A manager's ability to build a superior value proposition begins with learning to appreciate what drives a customer's willingness to pay for a product or service. That readiness is linked to *product differentiation*— the features of the product or service that enhance its desirability to

Box 1.2. Features of Competitive Positioning

1. **Product or service differentiation.** Understand the drivers of customer willingness to pay and ways to strengthen that willingness.

2. **Relative cost of production and delivery of the product or service.** Appreciate the key elements of cost in the supply chain, production, logistics, and marketing.

3. **Superior value proposition.** Identify the frontier where the combination of product differentiation and cost relative to competitors is optimal for the industry or market.

4. **Sustained value proposition.** Recognize that product innovation and competitive dynamics result in ever-changing superior value frontiers defined by the current leaders' combinations of product differentiation and relative cost.

the customer regardless of cost. The success of Apple Inc.'s iPhone, for instance, can be attributed in part to the distinctive combination of value, design, and functional features that increases customer willingness to pay a premium.[7]

The *relative cost* position for delivering products or services also enters into the makeup of a superior value proposition. The relative expense of producing Apple goods—the company's research and development, manufacturing and distribution, and branding and marketing—is high compared with the costs to produce rival products such as Microsoft's tablet. Similarly, Apple's cost of designing and marketing laptop computers far exceeds those of other competitors such as Lenovo and Dell. However, these higher costs result in products for which customers have a greater willingness to pay premium prices, more than offsetting the high relative cost position. However, firms with higher cost positions that do not have commensurate levels of differentiation end up at a competitive disadvantage to their more efficient rivals.

The trade-off between customer willingness to pay for products and relative cost positions for laptop computers by Apple, Dell, and Lenovo is displayed in figure 1.1. The figure shows that Apple's laptops are high in both differentiation and cost, placing the company closer to a frontier of superior value. Lenovo is near the frontier as well, albeit with lower differentiation and lower cost than Apple. Dell, by contrast, is significantly farther away from the superior value frontier than either Apple or Lenovo. As a result, both Apple's and Lenovo's laptops are better positioned by their managers for strong—though different—value propositions compared with Dell's laptops. The implication is that there is no single best position in a product market, but rather a superior combination of differentiation and cost compared with others in the market.

Strengthening Competitive Advantage

Given the internal and external factors associated with competitive positioning and value proposition, it is important to focus on decisions that create additional advantage for the firm relative to its market and industry. The ongoing goal of all players in a market is to provide superior combinations of differentiation and relative cost, and to place the product as close as possible to the best value frontier. At times the real challenge can be a continuation of the status quo; this lack of action results in a declining competitive position as rivals work to provide superior value to their customers. It is important to ask: What indecisions can result in a loss of advantage?

John Chambers, Cisco Systems' chief executive from 1995 to 2015, created additional competitive advantage for his firm in a number of ways, as we will examine in greater detail later in the book. He wanted Cisco to consistently provide customers with an end-to-end solution in the internet router business, including innovations in its components. If a customer sought a new component, Cisco would find a company possessing that technology. As a result, Chambers

Figure 1.1. Competitive Positioning in the Laptop-Computer Industry

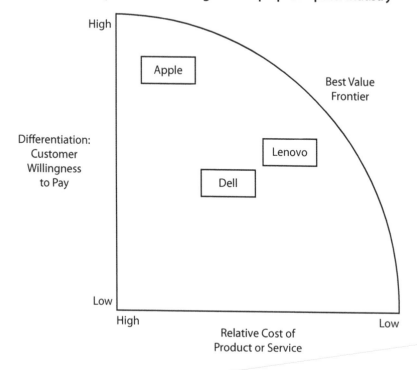

became a serial acquirer, averaging 10 purchases per year during his first decade at the helm; he repeatedly bought new technologies Cisco could not invent quickly enough on its own.[8]

Chambers had recognized the Achilles' heel of many technology-based service companies: their inability to consistently stay at the innovative frontier. He pressed his business managers to source technology when it was not available in-house, and he developed a unique postmerger integration process that bolstered the odds of success to 70%—more than twice the baseline rate of 30% across technology-intensive industries—by championing a faster and more effective integration than his rivals. His strategy emerged from a customer-oriented focus, and he had built a capacity to absorb innovation regardless of its source.[9]

In addition, Chambers's evolving intuition regarding what customers would come to want, regardless of what Cisco presently made, proved prophetic. Even in the wake of the 2008 financial crisis, when Cisco shares dropped by more than half over a five-month span, Chambers pushed himself to think about what was creating value for the firm and whether it could be sustained in the changing technology market. As part of that quest for advantage, he reemphasized a focus on customers in ways that would help him pinpoint and respond to market transitions and emerging technologies in advance of others.

A freefall in market share, or even a steady decline over time, offers a warning to a manager to consider a shift in strategy. But sinking financials is certainly not the only signal requiring a response, and many managers aspire to initiate strategic change well before all-out collapse. Market changes, shifting consumer demand, new entrants into the market, and emergent technologies can prompt managers to seek early redirection. Chambers, for his part, built his career on repeatedly anticipating such market shifts and readying his firm to embrace them, through both internal innovation and external acquisition.

Whether the company is Cisco, IKEA, or any firm competing for customers and market position, the strategy issues and questions in boxes 1.1 and 1.2 require management attention. But so do a corresponding set of leadership questions. To facilitate the integration of the strategy and leadership principles, each is framed to match a principle on the other side.

Principles of Leadership

We define *company leadership* as the actions required to enact and execute company strategy. Leading a company requires managers to devote time and intellect to the four leadership principles and questions in box 1.3.

Align People and Organization

Are the right *people and organization* in place to implement the chosen strategy? Does the top manager have the vision and means to execute the strategy? Are managers fully engaged and able to be a core part of the implementation? And does the organizational structure suit the strategy and enhance its execution?

Heptagon Micro Optics, a start-up based in Singapore, had mastered the arcane methods for making the tiny lenses that mobile

---

Box 1.3. Leading the Company

1. **Align people and organization.** Does the leader have the right people and organization in place to implement the chosen strategy?

2. **Create value.** How can the leader strengthen the internal factors that create or destroy value at the enterprise?

3. **Optimize advantage.** What actions can the leader take to optimize the firm's competitive advantage?

4. **Restructure for future advantage.** If the company requires a strategic redirection, how can the leader best restructure the organization for future advantage?

devices require for their cameras. After several rounds of venture funding, the company had become prosperous when smartphones emerged worldwide as must-have devices. But the company then hit a wall, unable to profitably expand even as demand for its products soared. Was it a faulty strategy that blocked growth? Or was the start-up's leadership at fault?[10]

Nokia Growth Partners (NGP), a venture investor, played the deciding role on whether to pull the plug on Heptagon or continue funding its money-losing operations. It appeared that Heptagon's management was responsible for much of the firm's languishing, not its strategy or even its technology, neither of which seemed terribly flawed. The chief executive had failed to streamline production, resulting in rising material costs and declining financial margins. He had opted for manufacturing methods that require long lead times, making tight-deadline delivery difficult. He had allowed his cycle times to lengthen, tying up working capital and forcing the company to invest more before it could sell anything. NGP concluded that it should double down on the company and its strategy—but remove its top leader.

Heptagon's new chief executive, Christian Tang-Jespersen, indeed added the commercial and human know-how his predecessor had lacked. "We found ourselves in a situation where we were making market-leading technology," the new CEO reported, "but not market-leading products." He informed his direct reports that the firm was facing a "catastrophe" and that they would have to place more trust in their subordinates and attack their hidden problems. The company would prosper, he insisted, only with more candor from the ranks. He empowered employees, permitting them to work at home and decide on their own holidays. He pressed for swifter decision making and shorter cycle times.

The previous CEO had arrived with credible credentials, including working experience in industrial electronics and semiconductor manufacturing. He also came as a cross-functional manager, with working experience in operations, sales, research, and development. But he had not come with a more complete headship package.

While Heptagon had been losing more than \$1 million per month under the old leadership, the new leadership turned the company around, and after four years it was *earning* more than seven times that amount. Its 4,000 employees came to ship nearly a million units per day, and in 2016 the company was sold for \$2 billion to an Austrian manufacturer, AMS AG. The value of NGP's holding in Heptagon soared to \$1 billion, more than five times its original investment.

Same company, same strategy—but new talent at the helm. The firm had gone "from the brink of bankruptcy," in NGP's own summary, to "a billion-dollar exit and the world's largest micro-optics supplier." Strategy plus leadership, it would seem, is an essential formula for performance, and we want to know what goes into it.

Create Value

How can a manager further strengthen the internal factors that create value at the enterprise? For instance, how might a manager better use the firm's assets, including people, market position, patents, technology, and even company culture, to create value for its customers, employees, and investors?

At Cisco, Chambers capitalized on the firm's culture of innovation and flexible organization to generate that value. Creative ideas were coming from too many locations, he reasoned, for a conventional pyramid to work in Cisco's market. As a result, he moved the organization's architecture toward a design that was less top-down, opening an upward path for more ideas to emerge from the ranks and across divisions, in effect allowing for more leadership of the firm to bubble up from below.

Chambers also learned to push for what he termed *collaborative management*: reducing hierarchy, working through teams, and using Cisco's own franchise product, TelePresence, for fast communication across work sites. New product decisions consequently came up more quickly from lower levels through newly formed cross-functional "councils." Information was increasingly shared through Ciscopedia, the Wikipedia equivalent for internal use, and major product decisions became the province of newly created lateral networks across some 500 senior managers. "The entire leadership team, including me," Chambers said, "had to invent a different way to operate." By the time Chambers stepped down as chief executive in 2015, Cisco had come to employ 70,000 and draw annual revenue of nearly $50 billion.[11]

Optimize Advantage

What actions can a manager take to optimize the firm's competitive advantage? At Cisco, Chambers and his team saw ahead of the market's changing value proposition to anticipate the emergence of free internet-borne voice service, long before Skype and others began deploying it. "Our non-telco customers were giving us clues that we just could not ignore," Chambers said. "We saw customers across the board beginning to shift away from proprietary networks, toward internet protocol-based networks. They were voting with their dollars." Cisco was already well positioned to build on its existing strengths and soon announced that its hardware would support both voice and data and that it would radically increase bandwidth for Voice over Internet Protocol.[12]

Restructure for Future Advantage

Finally, if the company requires a strategic redirection, how can the leader best restructure the organization for future advantage? This may entail anything from cost cutting to reinvestment, downsizing to acquisitions, or a combination of all these and more.

Chambers restructured Cisco a number of times to better position it for future advantage. After the internet bubble burst in 2000, for example, Cisco's business plunged, share price plummeted from $80 to $11, and Chambers laid off thousands. However, rather than retrenching for the long term, Chambers opted for the opposite, crafting a wholesale comeback strategy. The company moved away from a heavy dependence on a single product—routers for forwarding data to the right device—and organized for greater product diversity, including switches for forwarding data to the right network. Cisco's new switches were soon outselling its traditional routers two to one. Reorganizing had enabled Chambers to place his firm on a better path for executing its strategy.

Denise Ramos, the former CEO of ITT Inc., has a similar story. She had risen through the ranks at energy, food, and furniture companies, ever upward but always with the same function at her core. In 2011, when ITT split itself into three new companies, its governing board concluded that Ramos was ready to run one of the spin-offs. Though officially named ITT Inc., the new enterprise was better known around the water cooler as "Remain Co." It manufactured a variety of products—for example, vehicle brakes, shock absorbers, and water pump desalination systems—that did not fit the other two more-focused spin-offs.[13]

Ramos thought long and hard about the offer to become ITT's chief executive. She was in her mid-50s, a time when career choices are increasingly fateful. Company morale was terrible, dampened by the uncertainties of the breakup and "Remain Co.'s" second-class status. Doubts about job security and career pathways prevailed; even its solvency was questioned. With diverse divisions cobbled together, there was no shared history or distinct identity. "We did not know," she said, "who we were."

After she stepped into the role, Ramos launched workshops for the company's 10,000 employees; pressed for a more people-focused, less-numbers-driven culture; urged managers to better balance work and family life; and corralled her top team for brainstorming on how to foster a shared destiny. The goal, she said, was "to create an entity that people identified with."

To top off her challenges, ITT Inc. came with $750 million in potential legal obligations stemming from the exposure of workers and their families to the carcinogen asbestos years earlier. But Ramos pressed for growth, seeking to resolve the firm's obligations without sacrificing its growth drivers. Ramos also faced a crisis on the energy side of the business. ITT sold gas regulators and sump pumps to energy producers, and when the price of oil plummeted from $112 a barrel to below $30, customers simply stopped spending, costing the company more than $400 million in revenue. Investors and analysts questioned the firm's viability.

Undaunted, however, Ramos devoted five years to the company's restructuring, pulling divisions together, moving operations from one country to another, streamlining the workforce, and creating a new identity. By her last year in the corner office, ITT's annual revenue exceeded $2.7 billion, up from $1.9 billion the year before she had become CEO. From the first day of Ramos's work to the last, the value of the S&P 500 index had risen 123%, while ITT had climbed 161%. "We believe outgoing CEO Denise Ramos," wrote one equity analyst, "can take much deserved credit for defying the skeptics," leaving ITT, said another analyst, in "a very healthy position." Ramos had restructured well for future advantage.[14]

PART II

The Strategic Leader's Roadmap

Chapter 2

Integrate Strategy and Leadership

<u>The Strategic Leader's Checklist</u>

✓ **Integrate Strategy and Leadership**

O Learn to Lead Strategically

O Ensure Strategic Fit

O Convey Strategic Intent

O Layer Leadership

O Decide Deliberatively

Working with the strategy principles and corresponding leadership principles requires a departure from focusing primarily on strategy or, conversely, on leadership. By focusing only on the former, the role of human agency fades into the background, becoming a given rather than an active managerial challenge. By focusing only on the latter, strategic content remains too deep in the shadow of leadership capacities, neither disciplining nor directing their application. With both the strategy and leadership principles much in mind, it is essential to actively connect them.

The rationale for integrating strategy and leadership has been well expressed by the president and chief executive of the Estée Lauder Companies, Fabrizio Freda. He spoke to a group of 45 aspiring MBA students about what was required of his position within the firm, a company with some 48,000 employees in 2019 and annual revenue of $14.9 billion. He explained,

> My primary job as a leader is to help and encourage my team to think more strategically every day. What this means is three simple things.
>
> First, think what is it that you want to achieve. Develop a vision of your business and the results you want, and then answer the question: What needs to happen for this vision to become true? With the vision as your roadmap, then reverse-engineer a strategy to determine the critical changes that are imperative to accelerate in order to reach long-term objectives.
>
> Second, strategy is about choices. While making decisions to come up with a strategy, it is also important for leaders to recognize what not to change. I believe that the art of leadership is making choices and distinguishing what needs to change from what to protect and preserve in an organization. And once you have the vision and understand the multiple ways to get there—choose one.
>
> Third, strategizing is about the process of aligning resources and asking the question: Which capabilities do I need to make these things happen? Oftentimes we have strategic ideas, but if you don't have the capabilities or the strengths to realize them, you do not have a strong strategy.
>
> In summary, strategic leadership is about setting a clear vision and making choices of where to play and how to win, prioritizing goals, and ensuring you have the capabilities necessary to achieve those goals. If these elements are all in the discussion, this is strategic leadership, but if one is missing, success is limited.[1]

Freda's commentary on the integral combination of strategy and leadership is consistent with what we have concluded from our own research, interviews, and observations on companies in the United States and abroad. Integrating the two areas calls for a continuous and simultaneous discussion of both strategy and leadership questions (box 2.1).

In focusing on sustaining a superior value proposition, for instance, box 2.2 outlines how one might jointly frame the questions for integrating strategy and leadership:

Box 2.1. Integrating Strategy and Leadership: Two Key Questions

Strategy: How is our organization positioned to meet a given strategic goal?

Leadership: Do we have the right people, culture, and architecture in place to meet that goal?

Box 2.2. Integrating Strategy and Leadership for Superior Value

Product Differentiation

Strategy: How is the enterprise positioned in its markets, and how should managers respond to competitors, suppliers, and new entrants?

Leadership: Are the right people, culture, and architecture in place to implement that market positioning?

Production Cost

Strategy: What factors create or destroy value in the enterprise?

Leadership: What people, cultural, and architectural steps can be taken to increase value at the enterprise and reduce its loss?

Superior Value Proposition

Strategy: What are the optimal decisions for strengthening a firm's position and competitive advantage in the market?

Leadership: What are the most effective people, cultural, and architectural choices for achieving that position and realizing that strategy?

Sustained Value Proposition

Strategy: Is a different strategic direction required given
changes in the market?

Leadership: How should the firm's people, culture, and architecture be redeployed and restructured to achieve that new
direction?

For reflecting on these integrated strategy and leadership questions, we believe it is important for managers to consciously strengthen
their ability to address them and also to strengthen that capacity
within others for whom they are responsible. In the following chapter,
we identify three well-proven avenues for managers to fortify their
own strategic leadership and that of others in their organization.

Chapter 3

Learn to Lead Strategically

<u>The Strategic Leader's Checklist</u>
- ✓ Integrate Strategy and Leadership
- ✓ **Learn to Lead Strategically**
- ○ Ensure Strategic Fit
- ○ Convey Strategic Intent
- ○ Layer Leadership
- ○ Decide Deliberatively

Neither strategy nor leadership is a natural-born skill set, so learning to become a strategic leader is essential. We all benefit from beginning our study of both disciplines early in our careers, but learning to become a complete strategic leader is a life-long endeavor. So, too, is working to ensure that those who report to us are mastering the art as well. Academic research and management practice point to three avenues for developing the integrated understanding and application of strategic leadership, summarized in box 3.1.

We believe that each of the learning avenues is likely to be more effective when combined with an explicit and integrated emphasis on both strategy and leadership. Rather than a separate off-site program on strategy, for example, or a stand-alone program on leadership, a more optimal approach is to include a focus on both in all developmental initiatives. Each of these learning paths alone is

Box 3.1. Learning to Lead Strategically

- **Directed learning.** Engage in formal development programs with strategy *and* leadership components to strengthen one's strategic thinking and execution.

- **One-on-one coaching.** Pursue opportunities to receive guidance and feedback from mentors and professional coaches to improve one's strategic leadership.

- **Instructive experience.** Gain experience by taking on varied and increasing responsibilities and learning on the job what is most essential for thinking and acting strategically.

insufficient for achieving the required integration, but taken together, they constitute a potent foundation for learning.

The value of designing programs that use all three approaches can be seen in their widespread use among large companies in the United States and abroad. According to Aon Hewitt, a human resources and management consulting company that had conducted biannual appraisals of the leadership development practices of major corporations, the firms with the most comprehensive programs in the United States, Asia, Europe, and Latin America linked the content of their programs explicitly to their strategies. Aon Hewitt found that the top-ranked companies also arranged for executives, and sometimes directors, to actively coach or mentor the most promising managers and methodically assigned high-potential managers to a diverse range of developmental experiences.[1]

Directed Learning

Comprehensive directed learning builds on a long-standing leadership prescription, articulated by former General Electric CEO Jack Welch, that one of the most vital functions of company management is to ensure other managers learn to lead. Under Welch's tutelage, GE became a "leadership engine," investing in leadership programs, personal mentoring, and instructive experience to build its management cadres in ways that proved to be a source of sustainable advantage.[2]

General Electric established a management development center in Crotonville, New York, in 1956, and by 2013 it was reaching 40,000 GE managers annually. The company offered 1,800 courses and invested $1 billion in management development annually. The Boeing Leadership Center near St. Louis and Deloitte near Dallas offer similar programs to train their managers, as do American Express, IBM, and Procter & Gamble. Directed learning is also increasingly coming from a range of outside providers and online programs.[3]

One-on-One Coaching

Coaching includes one-on-one guidance and feedback on strategy and leadership from both informal mentors and professional coaches. The corporate universities of General Electric, Deloitte, and others often include personal coaching programs for large numbers of rising managers. They are intended to provide fine-grained feedback on an individual's existing capacities and her or his continued strengthening.

Andy Grove, who served as CEO of Intel Corporation from 1987 to 1998 and as chairman of the board from 1997 to 2005, had been coached earlier by Gordon Moore while at Fairchild Semiconductor International Inc., for instance, and Grove himself became a mentor to Steve Jobs in the late 1970s during Jobs's early tenure at Apple. Grove had also coached a generation of Intel executives and other Silicon Valley entrepreneurs including Oracle Corporation's Larry Ellison and Facebook Inc.'s Mark Zuckerberg.[4]

Instructive Experience

Directed learning programs methodically assign many rising managers to even more senior roles where integrating strategy and leadership becomes paramount, and this is where the third avenue for learning comes into play. Instructive experience involves a recurrent willingness to take on varied and rising responsibilities and to learn from those diverse engagements what is most essential for thinking and acting strategically.

The rationale for assigning increasing responsibilities to rising leaders as a learning method has been articulated by PepsiCo chief executive Indra Nooyi. When asked how she managed the stepping-stones a rising financial executive should take on the way to becoming a CEO, she replied, "You pick three or four people you think can be moved along and give them broad experiences. Not necessarily running a business, but put them in charge of big transformational projects or send them overseas. Give them experiences they would never have in the traditional CFO job and have them open their minds to all kinds of experiences, give them the ability to shape an agenda."[5]

Instructive experiences offer cumulative moments of reflection, and they can be further amplified by self-reflection on one's successes and setbacks. To examine the power of experience, we again draw on Cisco's Chambers.

A West Virginian with an MBA from Indiana University, Chambers earned a kind of traumatic postgraduate degree while employed at Wang Laboratories. Working closely with founder Dr. An Wang, Chambers experienced the company's abrupt collapse. In just four years, the firm had reversed from $2 billion in yearly earnings to a $700 million annual loss. At the time, the CEO of Wang Laboratories failed to appreciate and adapt to computer technologies that were fast evolving in the market, giving Chambers an eyewitness account of just how fatal such a strategic error could be. As a result, some 37,000 employees suddenly found themselves without a job, including Chambers. Wang's collapse convinced Chambers that no matter how successful an enterprise is at any moment, responsible executives have to anticipate disruptive technologies that can undercut or even destroy overnight what had been the firm's value drivers.

After Wang's failure, Chambers joined Cisco as senior vice president of worldwide sales and operations. The company— founded in Silicon Valley less than a decade earlier and named after nearby San Fran*cisco*—proved a good match for Chambers's new, failure-informed strategic thinking. With rapid promotion through the senior ranks, he reached the Cisco corner office just five years later at age 46.

Anticipating and preparing the organization for market changes—hard-earned strategic leadership principles that Chambers acquired from his days at Wang—Chambers undertook both internal innovation and external acquisitions, hallmarks of his early tenure at Cisco. He boosted sales in his first five years as CEO at an annualized rate of 57%. Cisco came to manufacture much of the backbone of the internet, and during its explosive growth in the late 1990s, it seemed that customers and investors could not get enough of what Cisco had to offer. By the company's own reckoning, at one point as much as three-quarters of the world's digital information flowed through internet pathways manufactured by Cisco.[6]

Then came the deluge. The internet bubble burst in 2000, and Cisco flipped from an annual revenue growth rate of 70% to an annual decline of 45%. The company laid off thousands, and its stock prices plummeted. It was Wang all over again—but this time without dissolution. Chambers was able to draw from his past experience, even though it entailed a monumental leadership error. Exceptionally difficult moments—when turned to informative advantage with after-action reviews—can thus serve as a particularly powerful, if dire, platform for learning to think and act more strategically in the future.

So Chambers plowed forward. He and his team crafted a wholesale comeback strategy and remade the organization based on a broader product line that included switches for forwarding data across networks. Before long, Cisco's new switches proved a hit, dramatically outselling the competition.

Welch had warned Chambers that "you'll never have a great company until you have a near-death experience." It was a painful prognosis at the time, but two years later much of Cisco's remake had been completed; Welch called Chambers again, this time to say that he headed a "great company" since he had weathered the crisis and, above all, learned from it.[7]

Under Chambers's strategy and leadership over two decades, Cisco became one of the most prominent enterprises in the United States. He multiplied the company's annual sales by a factor of more than 600, from $70 million to more than $47 billion. Dow Jones invited Cisco to become a component of its Industrial Average in 2009, and equity investors in mid-2021 gave it a market valuation of over $200 billion.

In summing up this experience, Chambers said, "You've got to be willing to just take the constructive criticism [and] learn from your mistakes, and then you've got to have the courage to change." And for that, he explained, you have to separate the self-inflicted errors from market-driven forces since leadership can only be strengthened by superseding the former.[8]

Although all three modes of learning—directed learning, one-on-one coaching, and instructive experience—are critical, it is important for managers to look to other instructional sources as well, including self-directed reflection. As a case in point, we return to Grove, who as a young engineer had been hired in 1968 to run operations for the newly formed Intel. He held a doctoral degree in chemical engineering but did not have a degree in corporate management, business strategy, or company leadership. Undaunted by his assignment to manage what he had not managed before, he used self-directed learning to "view himself as a student might: from outside," wrote historian Richard S. Tedlow, "peering down with the wide-angle, disinterested perspective of the observer."[9]

In a private notebook, Grove recorded his insights from both what he read and what he could see happening on the shop floor. A *Time* magazine article that he pasted into the notebook, for instance, diagnosed what made for great movie directors, reporting that they had the "vision and force to make" a host of "disparate elements fuse into an inspired whole." Grove queried in the notebook's margin, "My job description?" In another entry, he noted a growing appreciation for the fact that some of his employees were simply unable to grow as their jobs grew. Grove served as a lifelong self-directed student, repeatedly examining and absorbing his own experience.

Chapter 4

Ensure Strategic Fit

> **The Strategic Leader's Checklist**
> - ✓ Integrate Strategy and Leadership
> - ✓ Learn to Lead Strategically
> - ✓ **Ensure Strategic Fit**
> - ○ Convey Strategic Intent
> - ○ Layer Leadership
> - ○ Decide Deliberatively

Not every strategy can be led by every leader. An array of studies of executive succession and governing boards confirm the importance of ensuring that a manager is a *strategic fit* for the particular challenges facing the position. Instead of sourcing an executive whose leadership record is generally exemplary, company directors often seek an outstanding executive whose particular experience fits with the specific imperatives of the firm at the moment, similar to how a sports team looks to recruit and sign the best performers at particular positions of need.

Governing boards of firms facing financial challenges, for instance, are more likely to move their chief financial officer into the corner office; boards of companies tackling marketing challenges are more prone to bring up an executive from sales; and directors of companies looking to enter international waters are more likely to promote a manager with global experience.[1]

Box 4.1. Ensuring Strategic Fit

- **Work the data.** Gather data from those who are familiar with the position and the candidates to ensure a good fit.

- **Pinpoint priorities.** Evaluate the strategic and leadership imperatives of the position and, separately, conduct a similar assessment of the strategic and leadership capacities of the prospective candidates.

Strategic fit places a premium on a manager's ability to accurately identify the strategic imperatives of a position and then to correctly appraise the leadership skills of a candidate and whether the individual would make a good match with the position (box 4.1).

Work the Data: GlaxoSmithKline

In 2008, the British-based pharmaceutical company GlaxoSmithKline (GSK) held an open contest to identify a CEO successor.

Three years before the anticipated retirement of its CEO Jean-Pierre Garnier, who had led the company since 2000, the governing board began to work closely with the CEO and his top human resource officer to identify an optimal successor. GSK's directors and executives used the firm's strategy to prioritize their search for a successor by first articulating a comprehensive picture of what the industry would look like in the years ahead. Garnier, for instance, prepared a strategy paper on industry trends, with special reference to "cost pressures, growth trends, productivity, drug safety, and reputational issues, and how they might affect GSK." With that, he then identified a set of leadership capacities required in a successor, including industry knowledge, an ability to drive innovation, and a readiness for organizational change.[2]

Three managers emerged internally as CEO contenders for their demonstrated strategic fit with the company's imperatives. GSK arranged for the three to take on yearlong CEO-level transformation projects. Drawing on the finalists' performance in these projects and also on upward appraisals by 14 other executives who had worked with each of the finalists, the directors finally turned to their European pharmaceutical director, Andrew Witty, as the next CEO. Witty had been considered the least likely of the three finalists, but data from the special projects and upward appraisals brought him from dark horse to the fore as the best strategic fit.

Pinpoint Priorities: WorldCom

The features of a position and the facets of the candidates are many, and it is essential to identify the most vital features and facets for optimizing strategic fit.

WorldCom, the large telecommunications company, went bankrupt in 2002 as a result of criminal malfeasance at the company's top. It sought to emerge a year later from Chapter 11 under the name of MCI Inc. (the name of a company it had earlier acquired)—and under the leadership of a new CEO. To that end, the board sought a CEO who could reinvigorate a dispirited 60,000-person workforce, retain 20 million disaffected consumers, regain credibility with hundreds of corporate customers, foresee the emerging technologies that would carry the company in the fast-changing telecom industry, and restore a shattered credibility on Wall Street.[3]

The WorldCom board added to that all-purpose CEO description another dozen more specific criteria, ranging from having a proven track record running a multibillion-dollar company to turning around languishing operations and developing and executing strategy. An executive-search professional sourced four finalists for the position, and for each candidate he prepared a multipage summary that detailed a broad array of the contender's leadership capabilities. One candidate, for instance, was deemed to be a tough-minded and intense operating and financial executive. A second had held leadership positions at four global information-services companies. A third came with three decades of experience in the telecommunications industry. And the fourth had already led turn-arounds and was well versed in motivating large-scale workforces.

Identifying the two or three most important requirements for the position—and which candidate came with the best corresponding capabilities—proved inherently challenging because of the complexity on both sides of the equation. The documents outlining the WorldCom requirements and the four finalists' competencies contained extensive information, yet in the end, the directors had to reduce all of the information to a single decision: which of the four candidates to hire.

The directors concluded that restructuring the bankrupt company and its demoralized workforce would require above all a CEO who was not intimidated by huge challenges, came with a can-do attitude toward addressing the challenges, had a proven record of driving corporate change, could work effectively with technology managers, and was familiar with other company executives (since many of the firm's services were provided to other companies). Of the premier qualities of the finalists, the one candidate of the four with the most optimal fit by these position priorities and personal qualities was Michael D. Capellas, former CEO of Compaq Computer Corporation and then president of Hewlett-Packard Company. The directors selected him, and he in turn successfully restructured the company over the next several years and arranged for its sale to Verizon Communications Inc. for $8.5 billion, resur-recting a company that had been worth little when it had plunged into bankruptcy.

Chapter 5

Convey Strategic Intent

The Strategic Leader's Checklist
✓   Integrate Strategy and Leadership

✓   Learn to Lead Strategically

✓   Ensure Strategic Fit

✓   **Convey Strategic Intent**

○   Layer Leadership

○   Decide Deliberatively

Managers at all levels must be able to *convey strategic intent* if they are to effectively exercise strategic leadership. Whether chief executive or a front-line supervisor, a manager must be able to communicate the firm's strategic agenda in ways that are both unambiguous and persuasive.

While defining direction, managers refrain from detailing or micromanaging the specific enactments of the intent, though they certainly continue to hold their team members or subordinates accountable (box 5.1). Academics Gary Hamel and C. K. Prahalad articulated the value of strategic intent for business more than a quarter century ago, advocating for company leaders to offer a clear and sustained statement of company direction without detailing its execution. In one common phrasing, conveying strategic intent entails "hands off but eyes on."[1]

35

Box 5.1. Conveying Strategic Intent

- **Convey strategic intent.** Communicate the organization's strategic agenda with complete clarity.

- **Refrain from detailing how strategy is implemented.** Those responsible must develop a plan and execute it to meet the strategic agenda outlined.

The US Armed Forces has long advocated for commanders to appreciate and apply the integrating power of strategic intent. Senior officers are instructed to exercise leadership of personnel through clear-minded strategic instructions to subordinates and then enforcement of their "commander's intent." Because field officers often face uncertain, complex, and changing terrains in leading an operation, senior officers are called to clearly instruct troops in an operation's mission, objectives, and strategy—but then to let their trained and disciplined subordinates implement the strategy for achieving those objectives, making adjustments as required but without further guidance from above.[2]

The US Armed Forces later expanded this emphasis on the commander's intent to include "mission command," defined, in the case of the US Army, as "the exercise of authority and direction by the commander using mission orders to enable disciplined initiative within the commander's intent." The purpose is "to empower agile and adaptive leaders in the conduct" of their duties. In the injunction of the US chairman of the Joint Chiefs of Staff, the nation's highest-ranking military officer, service commanders "must understand the problem, envision the end state, and visualize the nature and design of the operation"—but then delegate its execution to their "agile and adaptive" subordinates.[3]

Two examples help make the case for the value of strategic intent for integrating strategy and leadership in business. The first comes from a calamitous event in Chile in 2010 and the second from the end of the Cold War in the 1980s.

A Seismic Shock

Chile suffered an 8.8-magnitude earthquake on February 27, 2010. The event, referenced in Chile as F27, released 500 times more energy than the earthquake in Haiti just six weeks earlier that had killed more than 200,000. The Chilean event was the sixth-highest-magnitude earthquake ever recorded, and NASA estimated that it moved the country west by eight inches and tilted the earth's axis by three inches. F27 devastated schools, hospitals, roads, homes, and businesses across a huge swath of the country's midsection, paralyzing the country for weeks.[4]

The economic damage was massive: Recovery would cost Chile the equivalent of 18% of its gross domestic product, nearly a fifth of what the entire country produced in a year. That was comparable to $2.7 trillion in economic loss in the United States, or more than 20 times greater than that inflicted by Hurricane Katrina in 2005, America's costliest natural disaster to date.

Chile's president Sebastián Piñera, inaugurated shortly after the earthquake, mobilized his cabinet to help the injured and bury the dead, then to repair hospitals and rebuild homes. He instructed ministers to restore damaged buildings and infrastructure on a demanding timeline, while detailing little about how they should proceed. He insisted, for instance, that his education minister arrange for all of the country's schoolchildren to be back in school within six weeks, yet offered little guidance on how to do so. The six-week goal was no small stretch, since one-third of the country's schoolhouses had been destroyed or severely damaged and a million students were without facilities. But within the president's unambiguous marching orders, it was then left to the minister of education to devise a solution.

Just six weeks later, the education minister had arranged for all of the country's 1 million children to be back in a classroom, albeit some in community centers, private homes, or even school buses. But the president's formula had proved effective: He had set forward his strategic intent and left his education minister to develop and execute a complex plan to achieve the goal on short notice, a plan that the president had neither the time nor the temperament to detail. Similarly, at the president's insistence, Chile's finance minister helped get the economy back on track within a year, implementing a plan to achieve a 6% annual growth rate at a time when the world economy was still reeling from the 2008–2009 financial crisis. The president proposed, but he let his ministers dispose.

Piñera's strategic intent did not stop with his country's immediate recovery. He also insisted that his ministers think long term, that the national comeback go well beyond what the country had in place before the earthquake, including stronger early warning systems, more resilient buildings, and better tsunami barriers. Piñera introduced a far-reaching strategic intent for national improvement, requiring his cabinet ministers to lay out and achieve a host of long-term goals for making the country more robust in the face of future calamities.

His long-term intent made clear, Piñera again left it largely up to his subordinates to execute, though his delegation of responsibility did not stop there. He took on the role of taskmaster, holding cabinet ministers accountable for achieving their goals in detail. He insisted they develop evidence-based options and make data-driven decisions, and he demanded that all of the specific targets in their comprehensive reconstruction plans be achieved on schedule.

The Power of "Tear Down This Wall"

US president Ronald Reagan had campaigned for the White House on a platform of challenging the Soviet Union, and while in office he repeatedly called for an end to the Soviet state. He expressed that intent through a host of sharp-edged but memorable phrases, implying that the Soviet regime and its Eastern European satellites were illegitimate. He asserted in a 1982 speech, for instance, that communism was destined to end up in the "ash heap of history," proclaimed the Soviet system in 1983 to be "the evil empire," and demanded in 1987 in Berlin that the Soviet premier "tear down this wall!"

To bring about an end to the Soviet empire—and the Berlin Wall—Reagan embraced a multipronged strategy for undermining the Soviet system, including a massive military buildup and a new space shield against Soviet missiles, neither of which the Soviet Union could afford to match. Beyond that, however, the president left it largely up to his White House staff and cabinet secretaries to turn his resolve into reality. With their unambiguous marching orders, they proceeded to do so in ways that the president could not have detailed; and in executing his strategic intent, they intensified the financial and ideological pressures on the Soviet system. The Berlin Wall came down in 1989, and the Soviet Union collapsed in 1991.[5]

In both Chile and the United States, the nations' leaders had set forward their unambiguous strategic intent. But each delegated its achievement to those on the ground who were in the best position to implement it.

Chapter 6

Layer Leadership

The Strategic Leader's Checklist

✓ Integrate Strategy and Leadership
✓ Learn to Lead Strategically
✓ Ensure Strategic Fit
✓ Convey Strategic Intent
✓ **Layer Leadership**
○ Decide Deliberatively

Strategic leadership should emanate from multiple tiers in a company or a country, not just the top rung. While the enterprise's strategic intent is conveyed by the most senior leader in the organization, it is then the responsibility of the managers populating the next tier to convey the same message downward and for their own subordinate managers to do the same in turn, with strategic leadership cascading down the company pyramid in what can be termed *layered leadership.*

Since leadership should not be seen as limited to the apex of an organization, in our view, vertical collaboration among the tiers in executing the top management's strategic intent becomes vital. The strategic intent of the top echelon must be faithfully conveyed and diligently enacted through each of the successive layers below, and then the several echelons must work hand in hand to achieve it (box 6.1).

Box 6.1. Layering Leadership

- **Convey strategic intent throughout the organization.** Each management layer communicates its strategic intent to the next layer down without micromanaging its execution below.

- **Work across layers.** Align and coordinate the work of the several layers, with managers in each layer supporting the work of those above and below.

- **Develop strategic leadership in all layers.** The downward conveyance of strategic intent and the effective collaboration among managers across the several echelons require development of strategic leadership among those in all the layers.

The power of layered leadership as a "mission multiplier" can be seen in NASA's actions when it successfully returned a badly damaged spacecraft, *Apollo 13*, to Earth after a near-fatal explosion in an oxygen tank. Three astronauts aboard *Apollo 13*, led by flight commander James Lovell, worked to preserve the few remaining resources left onboard after the explosion. Separately, the ground crew in Houston, led by flight director Gene Kranz, labored to ensure that the astronauts secured the resources necessary for reentry into the earth's atmosphere. Working in tandem, the leaders of the flight team and ground crew produced one of the golden moments in US space-flight history, the safe return of the *Apollo 13* astronauts—an outcome that neither tier could have achieved on its own but was achieved through the collaborative leadership of both.[1]

For layered leadership to work, however, leaders at each tier must possess the strategic leadership skills required at their respective level. If a lack of strategic fit or an inability to convey strategic fit occurs at any level, those below will not be prepared to execute the strategic intent from above, and the chain of layered leadership is broken. That is why the US Army places great emphasis on building agility and adaptability among its lower-ranking officers as a precondition for the senior commander's intent to be enacted.

Another Disaster in Chile

Mindful of a similar challenge of leading through layers, Sebastián Piñera, the president of Chile, had preselected his nearly two dozen cabinet ministers for their proven leadership records regardless of political experience, and he expected the same of them as they staffed their respective ministries. The power of this downward cascade of strategic intent through well-prepared lower tiers became evident when another disaster struck Chile just five months after the F27 earthquake in 2010.

Upon taking office, Piñera had designated Laurence Golborne as his minister of mining. Golborne was chosen not because he was especially familiar with either mining or politics—he was, in fact, experienced in neither—but because he had run Chile's largest retail chain, Cencosud. As company chief executive, he had overseen a workforce of more than 100,000 and an annual budget of more than $10 billion. Golborne had a proven record of strategizing and leading large enterprises, and it was those capacities—rather than his technical expertise or political experience—that the president had decided would prove essential in his own second tier.

A cave-in trapped 33 miners on August 5, 2010, in a shaft nearly a half mile below Chile's northern Atacama Desert. The next day, Piñera instructed Golborne that he should do everything feasible to rescue the miners even though they were trapped in a private mine over which the government exercised no direct authority.

The president's strategic intent made unequivocal, he left the subsequent decisions largely in Golborne's hands. The underlying premise for the delegation of that authority: Moving to the site of the mine, Golborne would be able to execute the president's intent about as well as anybody in Chile—and the president could add little further value from his office in the nation's capital to the many technical decisions required for their eventual rescue. Ten weeks later, Golborne and his team, their thousands of decisions disciplined but not micro-managed after the president had expressed his strategic intent, lifted the last of the 33 miners safely to the surface.[2]

Layered leadership thus serves as a vital connector between strategy and leadership. And in conveying downward the most senior leader's strategic intent, its effectiveness requires having put in place an ability for all layers to make decisions together. This can be seen in private companies as well as public agencies.

Apple's Rise to the Top on Layered Leadership

In formulating his principles for leading Apple Inc., founder and CEO Steve Jobs had put innovation at the center. One of his specific agendas was to create a "digital hub" for every private residence. He foresaw homes with linked music players, appliances, cameras, computers, telephones, security systems, and video recorders; Mac computers and their proprietary software would serve as connectors. All of the devices would be multifunctional, easy to operate, and aesthetically appealing. A new operating system, OS X, developed at a reported cost of $1 billion, would furnish the required interoperability and adaptability to subsequent generations of Intel chips.

Meanwhile, Jobs introduced devices for the digital hub one by one, each becoming a game changer in its own right. The iPod, for instance, displaced MP3 digital audio players with a smaller gadget that allowed for internet updating and a choice of songs. Serving as a first node in an ecosystem of related services, including iTunes, the iPod affirmed the potential of the digital hub strategy, knitting varied features seamlessly. Observers attributed Apple's build-out of the iPod and the hub concept more broadly to the vision and creativity of the chief executive, but it also depended on the leadership of layers well below him.[3]

Consider the role of Ken Kocienda, an Apple software developer whom the company had asked to create a virtual keyboard for the new iPhone. Given the mobile device's modest dimensions, the keys on the iPhone's virtual keyboard would have to be tiny, and for that, devising an autocorrect function would be essential so that users could type quickly and not have to backtrack to fix mistakes. Another challenge was how to cram letters, numbers, and symbols onto the phone's slender keyboard. Here, Kocienda's team came up with a toggling function, allowing users to easily switch the keyboard from letters to numbers to symbols, or even the Greek alphabet. Users readily embraced both innovations.

Kocienda's leadership of his engineering team's decisions—along with Jobs's leadership of his top team's decisions—proved foundational for the iPhone's launch. "The iPhone was an act of creativity," Kocienda said, but "it wasn't inevitable." Rather, it was an "accumulation of many small choices by a group of people working together closely in a specific time and place."[4]

When Jobs introduced Apple's iPhone in 2007, he anticipated it would be transformative for the company and even the industry. "Every once in a while, a revolutionary product comes along that changes everything," Jobs said. "Today, we are introducing three revolutionary products in this class. The first is a widescreen iPod with touch controls. The second is a revolutionary mobile phone. The third is a breakthrough internet communication device. These are not separate devices, it is one device and we are calling it the iPhone." The resulting product became one of the most successful technology combinations of all time, accounting for as much as half or more of Apple's annual revenue for years to come.[5]

Having successfully created the keyboard and autocorrect function for the iPhone, Apple then assigned Kocienda the role of developing a keyboard for the next big thing, the iPad. Kocienda brought in Bas Ording, a software designer who had already invented inertial scrolling, where a finger swipe can make a screen slide quickly at first but then slow down, a function that users found appealing and one that has become a standard feature on virtual screens. Kocienda's group sought to understand whether the new iPad keyboard should be a full replica of the Mac keyboard or just a subset of the Mac's keys. Kocienda worked with Ording and the team on a range of design concepts, converging on two prototypes. The first, a virtual replica of the full keyboard, would be familiar to Mac users. The second, which allowed users to switch the virtual keyboard from lowercase letters to capital letters and back, would be less familiar. They tested a range of sizes for the virtual keys and a variety of ways for correcting typos.

To determine which keyboard was better, Kocienda demonstrated his options to a room of top executives, including Jobs himself, in a conference room called Diplomacy at Apple's headquarters in Cupertino, California. As Kocienda entered the room, he saw Henri Lamiraux, vice president of engineering for iOS, the operating system created by Apple for its mobile hardware, including the iPhone, iPod, and iPad. Lamiraux reported directly to Jobs, coordinating engineering for the software and hardware interfaces for Apple products, and he served as a conduit between senior-most management and teams of engineers. Also present were Scott Forstall, senior vice president for iOS software engineering, and Greg Christie, head of the Human Interface Team. Here was the top layer, the big brass.

Kocienda displayed the two main options to them: the full Mac-like keyboard with smaller keys and the switchable keyboard with larger keys. In earlier demonstrations with other executives, Kocienda had found little agreement on the preferred option. As Jobs and the top team looked on now, Kocienda opened two screens on a prototype iPad. "There are two designs," he explained. "One has more keys, like a laptop keyboard, and the other has bigger keys," like "a scaled-up iPhone. We are thinking of offering both. Try the zoom key to switch between them."[6]

Flipping from one to the other, Jobs tested each of the versions several times. Revealing no emotion or preference yet, he turned to Kocienda. "We only need one of these, right? Which one do you think we should see?" Kocienda was taken aback, having assumed that this was a choice for the upper layer, not his own. With time for only a moment's reflection, he shot back, "I've started to like the layout with the bigger keys. I think I could learn how to type on it."

He added that the autocorrect feature already on the iPhone could easily be incorporated here. Jobs responded, simply but fatefully, "OK. We'll go with the bigger keys."

Behind the launch of both the iPhone and the iPad were several layers of leadership, with the CEO resolving the final issues but engineers like Kocienda reaching important decisions at their own levels. The formula for the layered leadership included clearly defined goals for each, frequent communications among the layers, a shared tempo to keep all layers on track, and continual feedback up and down the layers. For navigating the several layers, Kocienda invented his own roadmap: "Remove distractions to focus attention where it needs to be. Start approximating your end goal as soon as possible. Maximize the impact of your most difficult effort. Combine inspiration, decisiveness, and craft to make demos." Also, listen "to feedback from smart colleagues," and then, "creative selection moves us step by step from the spark of an idea to a finished product."[7]

Chapter 7

Decide Deliberatively

The Strategic Leader's Checklist

✓ Integrate Strategy and Leadership

✓ Learn to Lead Strategically

✓ Ensure Strategic Fit

✓ Convey Strategic Intent

✓ Layer Leadership

✓ **Decide Deliberatively**

The last of the six roadmap capacities to connect strategy and leadership is an ability to decide deliberatively: to make informed, analytic, and far-reaching leadership decisions. It applies to both the formulation and execution of company strategy.

The underlying concept has been framed by psychologist Daniel Kahneman, who distinguished between what he termed intuitive thinking and deliberative thinking. Intuitive thinking, he offers, operates automatically, works quickly, and draws on simple and concrete associations, including rules of conduct acquired from past events. Deliberative thinking, by contrast, entails initiating and applying intentional logic, often requiring disciplined and complex calculations, and it is built from both personal and abstract knowledge of past decisions and their consequences. Intuitive thinking leads to more reactive and tactical behavior, deliberative thinking to more proactive and strategic conduct.[1]

The more analytic tools of deliberative thinking focus greater attention on long-term decision consequences, leading to a more comprehensive evaluation of alternative options. Deliberative decision making becomes especially important during a period when actions are urgent and the stakes are high, because it is then that decision makers are confronted with a host of unanticipated choices, and careful assessment of the options and the final selection among them are likely to be particularly impactful for an organization.[2]

Intuitive processes work well when decision makers have copious data on the outcomes of different decisions, and recent experience is a meaningful guide for future actions. These processes may not be fully effective, however, during strategic redirections for which decision makers by definition have limited or no past experience. These are the moments when leadership decisions can also become especially thorny, complex, and risky—and thus more in need of deliberative thinking.

Without deliberative thinking, the high costs of initiating a new strategy might be seen as outweighing prospective gains, causing managers to avoid any changes; this is often referenced as a *status quo bias*. Also, managers tend to focus on the recent past in judging the likelihood of future events, a myopic view that researchers have termed *availability bias*. Analytic tools associated with deliberative thinking focus management attention on both short- and long-term consequences, leading to a more comprehensive and even-handed evaluation of alternative options (box 7.1).

To briefly illustrate, let's turn to a comparative study of the strategies of Apple, Intel, and Microsoft. Drawing on extensive interviews with former executives at each, researchers Michael Cusumano and David Yoffie reported that the firms under the leadership of Steve Jobs, Andy Grove, and Bill Gates drove their enterprises by setting distant and ambitious objectives. They expected company managers to work deliberately back from the distant goals to the present to identify the decisions that were required now to reach those future

---

Box 7.1. Deciding Deliberatively

- **Make disciplined decisions.** When facing strategic choices, make informed, analytic, and far-reaching leadership decisions.

- **Protect against decision biases.** In applying deliberate thinking to a decision, status quo, availability, and other biases are more likely corrected.

---

points. This obliged leaders at all levels to "look forward and reason backward," a leadership precept that others have termed "bringing the future into the present."[3]

In summary, integrating strategy and leadership, learning to become a strategic leader, ensuring strategic fit, conveying strategic intent, layering leadership, and deciding deliberatively should be seen, in our view, as an indivisible bundle—each component dependent on the others and all to be applied together. Yet conveying strategic intent from the top only works if each leadership layer is ready to lead in its own domain, and the leadership in each tier depends in turn on its cohort's ability to decide deliberatively. Taken together, these guiding principles for the integration of strategy and leadership constitute an essential roadmap, and all should be built into programs for strengthening a manager's or an organization's strategic leadership.

In part III, we look at the dynamic ways that strategy and leadership can flow from and reinforce one another. Both halves are essential, and the absence of either can prove ruinous. Firms that have well-developed strategies but underdeveloped leaders are likely to fall short, and firms with well-developed leaders but underdeveloped strategies are prone to face the same. We want neither facet to be deficient, and that calls for an enterprise to ensure both its strategy and its leadership are well developed and mutually aligned, neither one falling short or pulling against the other.

We focus on three challenges for ensuring that business strategy and company leadership can and do work together:

1. How enterprise executives actively transform their strategy into a business reality
2. How company leaders sometimes redirect their business strategy
3. How a new business strategy sometimes calls for new company leaders

PART III

Strategic Leadership in Action

Chapter 8

Strategy-Led Execution
Danaher's H. Lawrence Culp Jr.

For strategy and leadership to work together, to pull a firm in the same direction, company executive Larry Bossidy and management consultant Ram Charan have focused attention on the pragmatic concept of *execution*. This is the methodical means by which able company leaders work with a sound business strategy to create a well-performing reality.

Execution entails a systematic and orderly process that cannot be taken for granted. Effective execution does not follow automatically or flow readily from a firm's chosen strategy. Rather, it must be designed, implemented, and managed by those who lead the firm. In Bossidy and Charan's words, "Execution is not just tactics—it is a discipline and a system. It has to be built into a company's strategy, its goals, and its culture. And the leader of the organization must be deeply engaged in it." Execution is the leadership vehicle for transforming ideas into action, for bringing strategy into reality.[1]

Linking Execution to Strategy

A little-known but exceptionally well-performing industrial manufacturer, Danaher Corporation, shows the value of strategy-instructed execution. Founded in 1969 by brothers Steven and Mitchell Rales in Washington, DC, the company embraces a strategy of making higher-quality and lower-cost components than its rivals. Ordinarily there is a natural trade-off between product quality and production cost. But

Danaher sought to invert that historical compromise, placing an "and" rather than an "or" between excellent *and* economical.

To achieve this seemingly contradictory agenda of emphasizing delivery of quality with efficiency, Danaher's founders and succeeding executives turned to the concepts of continuous improvement and waste reduction. They created a Danaher version of process improvement that had been pioneered by Japanese manufacturers such as Toyota Motor Corporation. Danaher leaders pressed employees to draw on the concept of *kaizen*—change for good—both to better run itself and to accelerate growth among companies they acquired. They asked employees at all levels, from the front line to the executive suite, to continually improve all facets of developing, producing, and delivering their products and services with reliable, learnable, and repeatable procedures. They also required Danaher's business units to create their own, tailored versions of continuous improvement, further tightening the link between the firm's strategy and its execution.[2]

One of the founders' successors, H. Lawrence Culp Jr., inherited the kaizen system and doubled down on it. Upon finishing business school, he was drawn to a career in manufacturing, and in 1990 he joined one of Danaher's subsidiaries, Veeder-Root, which makes fuel dispensers and payment systems. He rapidly climbed the ranks, becoming executive vice president of the subsidiary in 1999 and chief executive of the entire corporation just two years later. As he rose, Culp concluded he could add the greatest value to Danaher and its acquisitions by staying with the Danaher version of the continuous improvement strategy but applying it even more rigorously and extensively. He strengthened, codified, and instilled the art of continuous improvement through what would come to be known as the Danaher Business System (DBS).[3]

Culp devised a library of tangible tools for Danaher managers to enhance product reliability and reduce product cost, both inside the legacy enterprise and among its many acquisitions. This could be seen, for instance, in Danaher's acquisition of Radiometer, a Danish enterprise founded in 1935. Radiometer produces instruments for measuring oxygen and carbon dioxide dissolved in arterial blood. Its instruments are widely used by hospitals for monitoring patients in acute care. Radiometer was already a world leader in a billion-dollar industry when a number of bidders stepped forward. As one of the prospective acquirers, Danaher managers walked Radiometer's plant floors for hours to study the potential for improvements through application of Danaher's manufacturing methods.

Culp and his team concluded that the DBS could indeed help Radiometer accelerate its growth worldwide. Radiometer executives were intrigued by the growth prospects, and Danaher acquired the company in 2005. To transform its strategy for the Radiometer acquisition into reality—to execute the strategy—Danaher scheduled an Executive Champion Orientation for 40 Radiometer executives to identify where research, development, and manufacturing could best be streamlined, in detail. They determined, for instance, that it took just 25 minutes to manufacture a small component of one product, yet the part drifted through the manufacturing system for 18 days as a result of unsynchronized procedures. Applying the DBS, Radiometer managers cut the part's travel time from 18 to just 2 days, a 900% process improvement.

While the contraction of handling time for a small component can seem simple enough for management, wholesale execution of the strategy through the entire manufacturing process required simultaneous improvements across four arenas: strategic planning, the DBS (kaizen), policy deployment, and intellectual property (figure 8.1).

The intent was to streamline the supply chain, reduce variance in product outputs, grow customer demand, improve company leadership, and strengthen employee capabilities. Much of the devil for each was in the detail. Danaher developed and anchored strategic priorities in specific initiatives throughout the organization. In the case of policy deployment, for example, Danaher stressed the creation of a "blameless" culture, where performance shortfalls were viewed as opportunities for root-cause analysis and management self-corrections rather than criticism of those responsible. This had the effect of incentivizing information sharing and shortfall corrections.

Figure 8.1. The DBS Training Modules

Business Process	Lean Supply Chain	Variance Reduction Tools	Growth Tools	Leadership Development	Associate Development
Strategic Planning	Value Stream Mapping	Danaher Materials Process	Voice of the Customer	DBS Immersion	Danaher System Training
Kaizen	Lean Conversion Mapping	Sourcing Workshop	Open Innovation	Root Cause Process	DBS Boot Camp
Policy Deployment Process	Total Productive Manufacturing	Six Sigma	Ideation	Danaher Leadership Program	Change Management
Intellectual Property Process	Lean Supply Chain	Supply Base Management	Sales Force Initiative		

Without details, business strategies run the risk of providing insufficient guidance for managerial decisions on the ground. Culp's experience at Danaher suggests how to overcome that limitation through a host of exhaustive leadership actions to execute the strategy. The company's strategy and his nuanced leadership proved a potent combination. During Culp's reign as Danaher chief executive from 2001 to 2015, the firm's market value outperformed that of the S&P 500 by more than a factor of two.

From Culp's experience at Danaher, we can also identify three operational questions for company leaders as they move from developing business strategy to actively executing it, summarized in box 8.1. The first question calls for managers' diagnosis of the value proposition for their products. The second invites managers to convert their strategy into a set of tangible actions to move the firm's products toward their optimal value frontiers. The third asks managers to delegate detailed decisions to their lower tiers, giving subordinates the latitude for implementation and inviting the upward flow of ideas for better execution.

Box 8.1. Execution: From Strategic Diagnosis to Implementable Initiatives

- **Determining strategic diagnosis and value proposition:** Have the key drivers of competitive advantage been identified, and has company strategy and its superior value proposition been compellingly set forward?

- **Defining strategic initiatives:** Has the company's strategy been translated into a set of detailed initiatives, and is there a plan to drive the strategy throughout the organization?

- **Identifying and developing operational leaders:** Has active execution of the initiatives been delegated to lower tiers, drawing on their ideas and providing them latitude?

Chapter 9

Leadership to New Strategy
*PepsiCo's Indra Nooyi and
Alibaba's Jack Ma*

The dynamic interplay between strategy and leadership calls for a manager's active redirection of the firm's strategy from time to time.

We have seen where this can go wrong. In the first decade of the twenty-first century, the demand for home video rapidly morphed in the United States. But the leaders of Blockbuster LLC proved unable to rewire their company's strategy from video rental to video streaming. At its peak, Blockbuster employed some 60,000 employees in 9,000 stores, but without a timely redirection of the enterprise, it filed for bankruptcy in 2010. By stark contrast, the leaders of Netflix, then an upstart competitor, had initially built their firm around a DVD-by-mail service but managed to convert that service into video streaming as the market moved into the internet. By 2020, Netflix was serving more than 160 million digital customers in 190 countries and had built a market value of $215 billion. A firm's strategy normally drives the kind of leadership required at the apex, but at pivotal moments like these, the causal arrow momentarily reverses so that a firm's top ranks can—and should—fundamentally revise its strategy.

Setting Up PepsiCo for Success

To have company strategy go right requires leadership for such moments of redirection. Indra Nooyi joined PepsiCo in 1994 as its chief strategist. Anticipating a declining market for fast food, she moved the company to shed KFC, Pizza Hut, and Taco Bell in 1997. Envisioning by contrast a brighter future in beverages and packaged food, she helped arrange a $3 billion acquisition a year later of Tropicana and then a $14 billion takeover in 2001 of Quaker Oats, maker of Gatorade as well as snack bars and oatmeal. Nooyi's strategic choices proved prescient, and as company earnings soared, PepsiCo's directors decided in 2006 that among a field of top executives Nooyi could best lead the company at a time when such choices were on the table. The board elevated her to become the fifth CEO in PepsiCo's 44-year history.[1]

Yet after becoming chief executive, Nooyi did far more than just execute the strategy she herself had helped develop over the years and the company now had in place. She concluded PepsiCo would have to further transform itself to continue growing. The company's markets were moving toward low-calorie beverages and nutritious foods, and the firm, she thought, would soon have to convert itself from snack food to health food, from caffeinated colas to fruit juices, from shareholder value to sustainable value.

Many questioned such a strategic redirection, however, since the company had long enjoyed widespread brand awareness and customer loyalty to its premier beverage, Pepsi, and an array of popular snack foods, including Cheetos, Doritos, and Fritos. Its chip subsidiary, Frito-Lay, had been growing dramatically as the company globalized its established product lines, especially in high-growth emerging markets. Despite those gains, Nooyi foresaw longer-term threats from the increasing health consciousness among younger consumers, who were becoming apprehensive about the impact of sugary drinks and salty foods on their own well-being and that of their children.

At the same time, Nooyi was concerned about the risks of building healthy drinks and nutritious snacks alongside PepsiCo's traditional and still best-selling beverages and foods. Many associates argued that the imperatives of near-term profit maximization still dictated an unrelenting focus on the firm's high-margin sugary drinks and salty snacks. Investing in healthier but less proven lines in the face of strong competition from Coca-Cola and food giants like Kraft Heinz, Mondelēz, and Nestlé could depress company earnings in the near term and perhaps even threaten the firm's long-term viability.

The beverage division—though committed to and still very dependent on its marquee offering, Pepsi—was already facing inroads from sports drinks and bottled waters and was thus more open to alternatives. It experimented with low-calorie beverages and rehydrating offerings with electrolytes. But Pepsi remained the company's most profitable product line, and archrival Coca-Cola continued to aggressively market its premier drink around the world. As a result, Pepsi's managers feared undermining their own profit drivers in a market already dominated by a formidable competitor.

The snack business presented an even greater challenge. Despite the high levels of salt and fat, or maybe because of them, its brands still commanded widespread customer loyalty. But Nooyi theorized that many of her employees, baby boomers and millennials especially, would themselves come to accept and even insist on healthier products if she could make the business case for the redirection.

Nooyi arranged a meeting at Frito-Lay headquarters near Dallas, Texas. She opened with a focus on company purpose and proposed a longer-term vision for the company that included product innovation in healthier categories—and a greater purpose behind them. At first, employee resistance was palpable. Healthier snacks would require starting new brands from scratch, impose large start-up costs, and distract from already successful offerings. As the meeting seemed to be heading toward a standoff, Nooyi asked each manager to ponder what kinds of new products would most motivate them to innovate.

Then, in a breakthrough moment, Nooyi asked Frito-Lay managers if they would be comfortable with their own children routinely consuming the firm's high-calorie and salt-laden snacks. She also asked them to consider the kinds of products that would give them the greatest personal pride in the company. The dialogue shifted from a focus on why a restructuring would not work to what new products could make it work, and the anticipated 90-minute encounter turned into a four-hour marathon. Nooyi's phrase for the redirection, "performance with purpose," took root.

The chief executive's new, purpose-driven agenda—one that still stressed performance—promised to give Wall Street what it required but also what health-conscious consumers sought. "It doesn't mean subtracting from the bottom line," Nooyi said, but rather "that we bring together what is good for business with what is good for the world." She created a language and crafted a culture that transcended what had long been deemed a zero-sum trade-off between profits and purpose.[2]

At first, as the new PepsiCo products came on line, they brought neither the scale nor the profitability of the firm's traditional offerings. Sensing vulnerability, Trian LLC, an activist investor led by Nelson Peltz, pressed the company to drop its healthier offerings. Some directors even questioned the redirection that they had earlier approved, and rumors of a governing-board coup surfaced.

But Nooyi held firm, gambling that her performance-with-purpose initiative was capturing employee imaginations—and in time would captivate customers too. Her company redirection was further emboldened when consumer activists rallied around the new agenda. She created new benchmarks to track the redirection, insisting that at least half of the firm's US revenue in future years come from healthy products such as low-calorie Gatorade and high-fiber oatmeal.

She also expanded the concept of consumer-focused purpose to include social purpose, though still requiring performance. The company under Nooyi's leadership focused more on renewable energy sources and campaigned against obesity. "People these days are bringing their principles to their purchasing," she said. And "we, in return, are bringing a purpose to our performance."

In 2015, PepsiCo removed aspartame, an artificial sweetener with adverse health effects, from Diet Pepsi, furthering the shift toward healthier foods. Witnessing the CEO stake her reputation and even her job on the addition of social purpose to profitable performance, employees rallied, and in the years ahead, the company delivered record levels of both innovation and profitability.[3]

As a result of the strategic shifts Nooyi had implemented at PepsiCo, Indian government leaders asked to partner with PepsiCo to create more nutritious lunches for schoolchildren throughout the country. India's government already subsidized midday meals that were reaching more than 100 million students every school day, and India's minister of food processing industries argued that his country's "children will be immensely benefited if such products are launched" by PepsiCo. He met with Nooyi to press for school fare for the entire subcontinent to be high in nutrition and low in sugar.

Nooyi's strategic redirection of the company proved successful despite currency fluctuations and varying demand that can make global growth challenging for any multinational corporation. During her service as chief executive from 2006 to 2018, Nooyi had grown her company's market value from $64 billion to $146 billion.

The Magic Words

For an even more extreme illustration of reverse causality—leadership to strategy—we turn to China's Alibaba Group and its founder and chief executive, Jack Ma (Ma Yun in Chinese).

When Ma visited the United States in 1995, a friend introduced him to the internet. Ma tested its utility by searching for a Chinese beer maker, any brewery at all, yet none popped up; however, he knew there were many on the ground in China. The internet promised extraordinary access, Ma realized, but at the time it still offered scant visibility into one of the largest markets in the world. The potential was huge, if unrealized. "I felt like a blind man," he recalled, "riding on the back of a tiger."[4]

On returning to China, Ma raised $20,000 to create a website that provided consumer access to small-business catalogs. But after an unsuccessful joint venture to build it out, he changed directions. He invited 17 friends to his apartment in 1999 in Hangzhou, 110 miles southwest of Shanghai, to create an internet-based service that would go far beyond the showcasing of beer, catalogs, and other products. He and his associates created a platform for small merchants to sell their wares, instantly transforming their market catchment from a city neighborhood to a vast continent.

When eBay Inc., the internet auction and shopping site, successfully entered the Chinese market three years later, Ma believed that its rapid growth posed a mortal threat to his business, and he acted accordingly. He created Taobao to link buyers and sellers via the internet, as did eBay, but with a different business model. eBay charged sellers a listing fee and collected a transaction fee when their items sold. Taobao, by contrast, billed neither sellers nor buyers for transactions, instead providing sellers with an advertising platform. Ma also concluded that the facilitation of internet-based transactions constituted the value-adding core of his strategy, and he accordingly outsourced almost everything else, including logistics, warehousing, inventory management, and even order fulfillment.

In 2004, Ma again broadened his strategic direction, adding Alipay, an escrow service to facilitate web-based transactions, allowing customers to inspect purchased goods with a money-back guarantee, and at the same time protecting sellers against defaulting buyers. In 2005, Ma accepted a $1 billion investment from Yahoo in return for taking over Yahoo China. Later, Ma created Tmall.com (formerly Taobao Mall) as a platform for branded retailers to sell their products on the internet at no cost. In 2015, Alibaba invested $4.6 billion in electronic retailer Suning Commerce Group Co. Ltd., giving it access to Suning's supply chain and 5,000 physical stores.

Ma expanded Alibaba's strategy recurrently as technologies emerged and markets evolved. He responded to eBay's Chinese entry with an online model based on different principles, bridged the inherent distrust between remotely connected buyers and sellers, and brought branded merchants into an online marketplace. In the face of challenges that could have destroyed Alibaba, Ma repeatedly revised Alibaba's business model, enabling his firm to raise more than $21 billion in a US initial public offering (IPO) in 2014, exceeding Facebook's $16 billion IPO in 2012. By 2015, Alibaba employed 35,000 people and had achieved a market capitalization of more than $200 billion, placing it among the top 25 companies worldwide, with a value that far exceeded that of eBay. By 2020, Alibaba's market capitalization soared above $700 billon.

PepsiCo and Alibaba illustrate the potential and the power of company executives who are ready to redirect their companies' strategies, sometimes repeatedly. Business leaders are often recruited to positions for which their experience and temperament are congruent with the challenges that the firm faced in the past and that shaped its strategy. And yet they should never be locked into that past; rather, they should remain ready to redirect their firm's strategy to better fit a changing landscape as the moment allows for it—and calls for it. Their application of the Strategic Leader's Roadmap is summarized in box 9.1.

Box 9.1. The Strategic Leader's Roadmap: Indra Nooyi, Jack Ma, and Leadership to New Strategy

- **Draw on leadership to redefine company strategy.** As leaders of PepsiCo and Alibaba, Indra Nooyi and Jack Ma redefined their firms' strategic direction and drove it through the ranks.

- **Advocate fit of strategy with leadership perceptions.** Building on the leaders' perceptions of their evolving markets, Nooyi and Ma laid out the imperatives for their firms' redirection in detail.

- **Convey intent to managers.** Both Nooyi and Ma developed the case for their firms' strategic redirection but left execution to their lieutenants.

- **Layer leadership to execute the new strategy through the ranks.** The leaders of PepsiCo and Alibaba pressed their lower

echelons to embrace and then enact performance with purpose in Nooyi's case and the internet's potential in Ma's case.

- **Decide deliberatively from revised imperatives.** Nooyi and
Ma asked their managers to make decisions that reflected the
overarching and long-term imperatives of their redirected
strategies.

Chapter 10

Strategy to Leadership
Cisco Systems' John Chambers

G iven a company's overarching strategy, its leaders inevitably have the task of adjusting and fine-tuning it, and that in turn requires evolving and amending their own leadership. The leadership skill set that is essential in an executive's early years will evolve as the market demands new kinds of products and services. Then, either the leadership team will be changed, or the leaders will change their own leadership.

Cisco's John Chambers opted for the latter.

Like all executives in rapidly shifting industries, Chambers appreciated the fact that Cisco technologies faced the constant threat of obsolescence. There was simply no assurance that even a dominant incumbent like Cisco could be sufficiently nimble to remain sustainably competitive. Though itself a maker of game-changing products, Cisco was always threatened with the same kind of disruption from others.

Chambers's early experience with the collapse of Wang Laboratories informed, or one might say haunted, his leadership at Cisco. Wang had been on top one year and extinct the next, the victim of fast-changing computer technologies that fleet-footed competitors had invented but Wang had failed to incorporate. Chambers vowed that Cisco would never suffer the same fate, but he also concluded that the company could never invent all the know-how in time to stay ahead of insurgents. The industry was too big, too innovative, and moving far too fast for his own R&D function to suffice, and he would thus have to acquire new technologies from outside his own walls.

With that in mind, Chambers adjusted Cisco's strategy to encompass a proactive search for new businesses emerging outside the company and a targeting of new technologies and business models. External acquisitions, however, came with their own well-known risks. Takeovers normally command a premium price for a buyer to gain full control, and research across many industries has repeatedly confirmed that just a third of all such acquisitions do more than recoup that extra cost. In addition, success rates for acquisitions in the technology sector have proved even more elusive since the target's human capital is more important but also more likely to exit soon after an acquisition.[1]

Having led the company's redirection, Chambers then instituted a new leadership scheme to execute the new direction, which included taking the established risks into account. Going back to one of the leadership questions we outlined earlier—are the right people and organization in place to implement the strategy?—Chambers identified more than a half dozen operating steps to optimize implementation of his growth-by-acquisition intent given its anticipated perils.

First, a proposal for an acquisition would have to be driven by the head of a business unit rather than a company executive. Those closest to a given market, Chambers reasoned, would better appreciate promising technologies than would top management. Second, team decisions, when the teams are well composed and well led, are generally superior to individual decisions, and a head of a business unit's proposal for an acquisition would therefore have to be vetted by a team of engineers, marketing specialists, and human resources managers before it would go to the CEO for final approval. Third, both Cisco and the target firm would have to share a similar understanding of how the industry is evolving. Fourth, Cisco and the target would have to have compatible cultures. Fifth, the acquisition would have to produce shareholder value in the relative near term, not only several years out. Sixth, the acquisition would also have to have favorable impacts on three constituencies besides investors: customers, employees, and partners. And finally, large targets would have to be headquartered near Cisco's home office in Silicon Valley.

Chambers had learned that all of these leadership principles were valuable for overcoming the high risks of being a serial acquirer. However, knowing that none were sacrosanct, he insisted that a target for takeover meet at least three and preferably four of these criteria but not necessarily all.

After the acquisition concluded, Chambers required additional steps to facilitate the new firm's integration into Cisco. Again, instructive experience warned him that however strategically promising an acquisition, integration of the acquired firm too often languished in the months after the money changed hands. And in cases where the strategic fit was less than perfect or the price was exceptionally high, it was all the more important that integration be engineered quickly and smoothly since the margin for error would be smaller.

For incorporating an acquired firm, Chambers insisted that Cisco follow a fast, codified, and repeatable process for bringing the target—both people and products—into Cisco's way of doing business. Research on acquisitions has shown that shortcomings in the incorporation process tend to be a major stumbling block (the strategy driving the acquisition is not accompanied by timely leadership of the acquisition), and Chambers concluded that fast and full integration would be critical. He insisted freshly acquired employees receive new work titles, job descriptions, business cards, and email accounts the next day. He stipulated that those in functions such as sales and marketing be fully incorporated into Cisco's equivalent functions.

Occasional speed bumps forced Chambers to rethink his acquisition strategy and leadership. When Cisco's stock declined precipitously after the internet bubble burst in 2000, for instance, the company could no longer use its stock as a currency for acquisitions. When domestic demand for internet hardware plummeted, Chambers turned to acquisitions outside of the company's traditional focus on internet infrastructure, entering new fields such as videoconferencing, internet security, home networking, and wireless switching.

Some bumps for Chambers were just plain bumps. For instance, he purchased Pure Digital Technologies in 2009 for $590 million, a foray into the consumer electronic business, but in the end it added little value to Cisco. The target's popular video camera—the Flip—soon gave way to smartphones with better high-definition capacities, and just two years later Cisco closed the camcorder business and severed its 550 employees.

Despite the occasional setback, the consistency over time and the broad scope of Chambers's evolved and learned leadership for acquisitions are evident in table 10.1, displaying Cisco's acquisitions from 2000 to 2005, and table 10.2, showing Cisco's 10 largest purchases over the two decades of Chambers's leadership.

With a strategy of acquisitions that included actively leading their integration, Chambers worked to keep his company ahead of the frequent changes and disruptions in its markets. And in doing so, he defied the odds of technology acquisitions, achieving a success rate near 70%, double the normal rate. He moved the company in new directions that its own R&D might not have been able to anticipate or invent. His foray into high-definition teleconferencing, for example, came through the company's $3 billion purchases of WebEx in 2007 and Tandberg in 2010 as part of its emergent strategy of servicing the internet of things. At the same time, it should be noted, Chambers also invested in Cisco's own R&D function on the premise it could incubate some technologies the market might otherwise ignore. Cisco established a facility near San Francisco to house engineers and developers who would work on new venture ideas in a setting with the ambience of a start-up.

Table 10.1. Cisco's Acquisitions, 2000–2005

Date	Company	Market
2000		
January 19	Compatible Systems Corp.	Service Provider VPN Solutions
January 19	Altiga Networks	Enterprise VPN Solutions
February 16	Growth Networks Inc.	Internet Switching Fabrics
March 1	Atlantech Technologies Ltd.	Network Element Management Software
March 16	JetCell Inc.	In-building Wireless Telephony
March 16	InfoGearTechnology Corp.	Software to Manage Information Appliances
March 29	SightPath Inc.	Content Delivery Optimizers
April 11	PentaCom Ltd.	Metro IP Networks
April 12	Seagull Semiconductor Ltd.	High-speed Silicon for Terabit Routers
May 5	ArrowPoint Communications Inc.	Content Networking Technology
May 12	Qeyton Systems	Metropolitan DWDM Technology
June 5	HyNEX Ltd.	ATM and IP solutions
July 7	Netiverse Ltd.	Content Aware Switches
2000		
July 25	Komodo Technology Inc.	Voice-over-IP (VoIP) Devices for Analog Phones
July 27	NuSpeed Internet Systems Inc.	IP-enable Storage Area Networking Technology
August 1	IPMobile Inc.	Mobile Wireless Internet
August 31	PixStream Inc.	Distribute and Manage Digital Video
September 28	IPCell Technologies Inc.	Voice and Data Integrated Access Services
September 28	Vovida Networks Inc.	Voice over IP (VoIP)
October 20	CAIS Software Solutions	Broadband Service Management Solutions
November 10	Active Voice Corporation	Unified Messaging

(continued)

Table 10.1. (cont.)

Date	Company	Market
November 13	Radiata Inc.	Wireless LAN
December 14	ExiO Communications Inc.	Wireless Networks
2001 July 27	Allegro Systems	Virtual private networks
2002		
May 1	Hammerhead Networks	Computer networking
May 1	Navarro Networks	Computer networking
July 25	AYR Networks	Computer networking
August 20	Andiamo Systems	Data Storage
October 22	Psionic Software	Intrusion detection
2003 January 24	Combinet Inc.	Intrusion detection
March 19	Internet Junction Inc.	Intrusion detection
March 20	Grand Junction Networks Inc.	Echo cancellation
November 12	Network Translation Inc.	Computer networking
2004 March 12	Twingo Systems	Computer security
March 22	Riverhead Networks	Computer security
June 17	Procket Networks	Routers
June 29	Actona Technologies	Data Storage
July 8	Parc Technologies	Routers
August 23	P-Cube	Service delivery platform
September 9	NetSolve	Information technology
2004 September 13	Dynamics.soft	Communication software
October 21	Perfigo	Computer networking

Table 10.1. (cont.)

Date	Company	Market
November 17	Jahi Networks	Network management
December 9	BCN Networks	Routers
December 20	Protego Networks	Network security
2005 January 19	Compatible Systems Corp.	Service Provider VPN Solutions

Source: Singh, Chaudhuri, and Shelton, 2008a, 2008b.

Table 10.2. Cisco's 10 Largest Acquisitions, 1996–2015

Rank	Target	Market	Price	Year
1	Scientific-Atlanta	Digital Cable TV Boxes	$6.9 billion	2005
2	Cerent Corporation	Synchronous optical switching	$6.9 billion	1999
3	Arrowpoint Communications	LAN switching	$5.7 billion	2000
4	NDS Group	Conditional access	$5.0 billion	2012
5	StrataCom	ATM switching	$4.0 billion	1996
6	Tandberg	Videoconferencing	$3.3 billion	2010
7	WebEx	Web Conferencing	$3.2 billion	2007
8	Starent Networks	Mobile IP Networks	$2.9 billion	2009
9	Sourcefire	Computer security	$2.7 billion	2013
10	Andiamo Systems	Data storage network switching	$2.5 billion	2002

Source: Public sources and company announcements.

Active execution of strategy calls for leaders to be fully engaged. But that engagement, as we have seen at Cisco, does not mean controlling from the corner office. Rather, it depends on the leader's learning and then setting forward a superior value proposition, making his or her intent clear, listening for ideas from lower tiers,

Box 10.1. The Strategic Leader's Roadmap: John Chambers and Strategy to Leadership

- **Draw on strategy to define company leadership.** John Chambers committed himself to developing an organization that combined customer centricity with product innovation, and he disciplined his selection of company leaders around this agenda.

- **Advocate fit of leadership with strategy.** Strategic priorities informed by customer demand drove Chambers's talent development and management retention.

- **Convey intent to managers.** Chambers insisted his managers focus on end-to-end and innovative solutions for customers using internet routers, networking equipment, and associated hardware and software, seeking the best solutions.

- **Layer leadership to execute strategy through the ranks.** Chambers devolved authority to leaders in the lower levels to propose and build new solutions for customers either internally or through acquisitions.

- **Decide deliberatively from strategic imperatives.** Chambers insisted that product decisions reflect the longer-term needs of his customers and the long-term strategy of the company.

---

specifying a limited set of specific initiatives, and then delegating execution to operational leaders who have embraced the leader's agenda.

Chambers had driven Cisco's operations for over two decades. In his leadership role, he embraced the company's strategy when he first became its chief executive and led its implementation over the years, but as his markets and their technologies evolved, he learned through instructive experience to lead the company in new ways. His own application of the Strategic Leader's Roadmap is summarized in box 10.1.

PepsiCo, Alibaba, and Cisco provide examples of company leaders who moved with agility in their application of strategy and leadership both individually and in combination, evolving each as markets demand. It is a high-wire act and one that occurs with some regularity. The learned eye can see it, and leaders who are life-long learners should be better prepared to do it.

PART IV

Strategic Leadership at the Board and Investor Levels

Chapter 11

Strategic Leadership for Boards and Investors

Top management is the main driver of a firm's strategy and leadership, but there are two other high-stakes players: the firm's directors and investors. The rising salience of strategic leadership can be seen in the expanding role of company directors in exercising strategic direction of the enterprise and in the growing power of investors demanding effective leadership from the enterprise.

Like managers, company directors and investors must learn to answer the key questions for integrating strategy and leadership referenced in chapter 2 to perform their own expanded oversight function.

1. Do company executives *and* directors have a compelling strategy for creating value and increasing advantage?
2. Are company executives and directors capable of thinking and acting strategically?
3. Is the firm's organization capable of executing its strategy?
4. Do all executives and directors add value to the company's strategy and leadership?

In this chapter, we focus on the increasing engagement of directors and investors, and we show how globalization is driving some of that change. In the following chapter, we concentrate on the increasing influence of investors on company strategy and leadership.

Changing Oversight

In decades past, corporate directors would have displayed little interest in either strategy or leadership of their company. In business school professor Jay Lorsch's biting appraisal, most nonexecutive directors had been more "pawns" than "potentates," and most investors had embraced the Wall Street Rule: If you don't like a company's strategy or leadership, don't intervene, sell the stock. Directors and investors were of course served—or sometimes disserved—by a firm's strategy and leadership, but they lacked the wherewithal or interest to influence either.[1]

A capacity for directors and investors to exercise influence on a firm's strategy and leadership, however, emerged in recent years as the bulk of equity stakes in large US firms flowed from millions of individual holders into the hands of just several thousand professionals. In 1950, 6% of the equity in publicly traded firms was held by institutional investors, but by the end of the century that fraction had grown tenfold.

The ownership concentration was driven by a seemingly inexorable rise of managed retirement accounts, pension funds such as the California Public Employees' Retirement System and Teachers Insurance and Annuity Association, and investment companies such as BlackRock, Fidelity Investments, State Street Corporation, and Vanguard Group. With company ownership far more concentrated among a relatively small set of money managers, professionals learned through instructive experience that they could press companies to strengthen strategies or improve leadership through proxy fights, takeover threats, and media campaigns.[2]

At the same time, equity investors, public regulators, and governance raters also pressed for strengthened boards so that directors could exercise their influence directly on company strategy and leadership. The Sarbanes-Oxley Act of 2002, the New York Stock Exchange rules of 2003, and the Dodd-Frank Wall Street Reform and Consumer Protection Act of 2010 added regulatory measures for further doing so. One of the most fateful measures was a Sarbanes-Oxley provision that boards designate a lead director, defined as an independent, nonexecutive board member who would take responsibility for the board's operations and decisions if the company's chief executive and board chair were one and the same. This had the unintended effect of creating a spearhead for the board who could focus directors' attention on the firm's strategy and leadership. Like managers who have learned to think and act strategically, directors have as a result also worked to learn how to think and act strategically. These developments have not been unique to US enterprises, and we have found similar trends in other countries, including China and India.[3]

As governing boards are morphing from passive and ceremonial to active and substantive, directors are also more directly engaged in their firms' international strategy and leadership since most major firms are becoming more global in their operations and sales.

The Board of Lenovo Group

China's Lenovo Group, the world's largest personal computer company, illustrated the changing role of its board as it globalized its operations. Directors played a central role in defining company strategy, leadership, and their integration for the company's globalization.[4]

Founded in 1984, Lenovo emerged two decades later as China's largest computer maker, securing 27% of the nation's rapidly expanding computer market and earning annual revenue of more than $3 billion. By 2004, though, Lenovo's rapid sales growth was beginning to flatten, in part because of strong domestic inroads by US competitors Hewlett-Packard Co. and Dell. Lenovo executives concluded that long-term expansion depended on becoming an international player, just as many US and European companies had concluded in years past. "In our world," explained chief executive Yang Yuanqing, "a high growth rate is hard to sustain if you only try to maintain your position in the China market."[5]

On December 7, 2004, at a Beijing news conference attended by approximately 500 Chinese and Western journalists, Lenovo announced it was acquiring IBM's personal computing division for $1.75 billion. In the wake of the acquisition, Lenovo actively embraced the four questions in box 1.3 (chapter 1) to strengthen the leadership of its directors. On the second issue, for instance— are all board members adding value to the company's strategy and leadership?—the company revamped its board's membership and procedures to strengthen the directors' multinational contributions. On the first and third issues—are the post-acquisition governing board and top team aligned and prepared to think and act strategically to optimize the firm's positioning in the computer market?—director attention expanded to focus on the strategy and leadership of the company's multinational operation.

First, the revamping: In 2003, the year before the IBM purchase, nonindependent directors outnumbered independent directors four to three. The post-acquisition board, by contrast, was divided among five executive directors, three private equity directors, and three independent directors. Before the acquisition, all seven of the directors were Chinese or of Chinese origin. After the acquisition, 4 of the 11 directors were Americans. Before the acquisition, board meetings were always conducted in Chinese, but afterward English became the medium. Going into the acquisition, both the executive chairman and the chief executive were Chinese; coming out of the acquisition, the executive chairman was Chinese and the CEO was American. Ma Xuezheng, the company's CFO at the time of the acquisition, declared, "This is going to be very much an international company operated in an international fashion." That now carried into the boardroom.

The decision to add international directors was intended to incorporate global expertise into the boardroom and to help the Chinese and American teams work together. Nonexecutive director Shan Weijian explained, "We don't want people to have a feeling of takeover [by a] Chinese company of the American company. We want an integration process [that] doesn't involve which part takes which."[6]

After the acquisition, Lenovo's directors pressed for bringing new directors onto the board who would add deep experience to the firm's strategy and corporate leadership. The selection standards for new board members, reported Yang, now came to include both executive experience and strategic vision. For one board seat, for instance, the company vetted more than 20 candidates, narrowed the list to 4 finalists, and finally invited John Barter, who had served as AlliedSignal's chief financial officer and president of its 35,000-employee automotive division. He was chosen because of his proven experience in leading a large profit-and-loss company division.

Regarding the greater engagement of Lenovo's directors in its strategy and leadership: In the wake of the IBM PC acquisition, Lenovo moved its directors from a relatively limited role in monitoring management to more active engagement in the company's strategy and leadership. "The IBM PC acquisition is a watershed," said Lenovo founder and executive chair Liu Chuanzhi. "Before that point," he said, "the board of directors did not play much" of a role. The board had been primarily concerned with audit and compensation, but after the acquisition it would come to play a far larger role.

The strengthening of the Lenovo board brought directors into direct guidance of the integration strategy for merging Lenovo's and IBM's distinct operating styles. IBM had built a business model around strong enduring relations with select corporate customers; Lenovo, by contrast, had created a more transactional model with many retail customers. Although large-enterprise relationships had been the staple of IBM's PC sales, Lenovo management anticipated greater global growth on the retail side, and it sought strategic guidance from the company's reconstituted board on optimal opportunities for building that model abroad.

To ensure a disciplined alignment of strategy and leadership, Lenovo formed a board-designated strategy committee, charged with vetting the company's mid- and long-term decisions on behalf of the directors. It included two Chinese executive directors (Yang Yuanqing and Liu Chuanzhi) and two American nonexecutive directors (James Coulter, a founding partner of the private equity firm Texas Pacific Group, and William Grabe, a managing director of private equity firm General Atlantic).

The Lenovo board met quarterly, but the strategy committee met monthly on issues ranging from company direction to cultural integration. The committee served as an "impartial third party," reported executive chair Yang, to help prevent a "confrontation" between the Chinese- and American-heritage divisions of the company. In the experience of CEO William Amelio, the directors worked with him and the other executives to pick from an array of choices "the right idea that is going to maximize the core competence of the company."

The Lenovo directors also became directly engaged in decisions on executive succession—the key choices on the company's leadership, an arena that had not been the board's prerogative before the IBM PC acquisition. The two independent directors from the private equity groups—Coulter and Grabe—played a pivotal role, for instance, in the early replacement of the first CEO after the IBM acquisition. At the time of the transaction, IBM's Stephen Ward had seemed the logical candidate for the role of chief executive, with Yang to serve as executive chairman, but within several months it was evident to the board's strategy committee that Ward's leadership was not a good fit with the firm's new direction. Supply chain efficiencies would be critical to ensure the profitability of the combined companies, but the first CEO did not come with the requisite experience for optimizing those efficiencies in an extremely cost-conscious market.

In applying the third set of the four management questions in box 2.2 (chapter 2) for integrating strategy and leadership—are the top team and governing board capable of thinking and acting strategically now in the far more international market for its products?—the board pressed for Lenovo's officers to reflect the new geographies where the company now operated. Of the top management team in 2004, a year before the acquisition, all were Chinese; of the 18 members of the top management team in 2007, two years after the purchase, 6 were from greater China, 1 from Europe, and 11 from the United States.

Here again, the directors' expertise on strategy and leadership proved instructive. Yang and Liu worried that an early and unexpected exit of the top US executive from the newly combined companies would cast a shadow over the strategy of globalizing the firm. Neither Yang nor Liu knew the international computer industry well enough to identify a replacement with the requisite leadership skill set, and they turned to directors Coulter and Grabe to source several candidates for succession, including William Amelio, then head of Dell's Asian operation, who became the successor. The directors even contributed their expertise to managing the replacement. Yang and Liu were unfamiliar with the process of relieving a US CEO, but Coulter and Grabe were. One of them explained, "We have done this repeatedly, and we are familiar with the US market and the practice over there, the environment, and how to do it."

Our interviews with Lenovo executives and directors revealed that a host of other strategic issues came before the board for its vetting and final decision making. Those issues included how long to retain the IBM logo on its products (the acquisition agreement had allowed for five years), what new acquisitions to pursue, which adjacent product areas to enter, and whether to build devices that bridge laptops and desktops. The strategy committee in particular went "through all the options and thoroughly [vetted] the pros and cons of the various courses of action," said Amelio. The two American directors from the private equity firms brought extensive experience in acquisitions, making them particularly valuable for appraising prospective decisions, in the experience of Amelio. They were "totally invaluable," he said, "because the name of their game is lots of acquisitions and mergers."

When Lenovo executives considered acquiring another personal computer maker, the strategy committee and even the full board became actively engaged on whether to proceed and, if so, what to pay. "Everybody was involved," reported nonexecutive Shan Weijian, "because this is a large issue for the entire company." Lenovo decided to back off, guided by the board's skepticism about the deal's potential value.

The strategy committee also played a particularly important role in appraising the company's leadership. The executive chair and the chief executive submitted annual self-assessments and 360-degree feedback results to the committee and the board, and the directors then evaluated the extent to which the executives had achieved their annual plan's financial, market-share, talent recruitment, and related goals.

We have seen a sharp divide between the way the Lenovo board operated before and after its decision to build out globally with the IBM PC division acquisition. Before the purchase, the board had operated without a strategy committee or an annual performance review. Now it had both. And whereas director decisions had previously been limited to mostly accounting audit and shareholder rights, now their decisions ranged from branding to sourcing, and more generally from strategy to leadership.

Directors played a far larger role in both company strategy and leadership in the wake of the IBM acquisition. They had replaced the first chief executive, decided against an acquisition, and facilitated cross-cultural integration of widely different divisions. A decade after the IBM PC acquisition and remake of its board and management to better strategize and lead the company, Lenovo's global market share of PC sales had become the largest of all competitors, ahead of America's Hewlett-Packard and Dell and Taiwan's Acer.

As we witnessed at Lenovo, directors of large companies in many countries are becoming increasingly involved in questions of strategic leadership, and we anticipate that directors will more forcefully define company strategy and leadership in the years ahead.

Chapter 12

Investor Demand for Strategic Leadership

Professional investors have not always been content to allow company boards on their own to press companies to optimize their strategies and leadership. Activist holders have increasingly opted to press more directly themselves, demanding changes in strategy or leadership and sometimes both by threatening—and even winning—seats on the board, despite the fact that activist investors rarely hold more than a thin slice of a company's stock.

Investors, whether activist or just institutional, face the same set of concerns as directors. They are just a step removed. They once had little choice but to sell their holdings in a publicly listed company if its strategy or leadership did not measure up. Today, because of the concentration of equity holdings in the hands of professional money managers and the strengthening of directors' hands in setting company strategy and selecting company leadership, investors exercise increasing influence.

The presence of several hundred activist firms, some sitting on more than $20 billion by 2021, has meant that few American companies, even the largest, remain immune to activist campaigns. Among those targeted have been Apple, Microsoft, and even a well-performing DuPont. With a market value of $65 billion, 58,000 employees, and a share price outperforming the S&P 500 index over the prior two years by 47%, DuPont came under the crosshairs of Trian Fund Management LP.[1]

With more than two centuries of making everything from gunpowder to nylon and Tyvek, DuPont had changed strategy and leadership many times. But Trian, led by Nelson Peltz, demanded the company spin off low-growth divisions and cut costs by $4 billion. And to force the changes, Trian asked for four board seats of its own choosing. Trian held only 2.4% of DuPont's stock, but the challenge proved forceful as many institutional investors backed it; however, Trian fell short of garnering the required majority of votes for placing its candidates on the board. In the wake of the investor pressures, DuPont directors changed company leadership, ousting the CEO, and changed company strategy, agreeing to merge with the Dow Chemical Company and have the combined firms redivide, as the challenging investor had been demanding. The *Wall Street Journal* headlined the merger, "Dow, DuPont Deal Cements Activists' Rise."[2]

Another activist investor resoundingly proved that it could replace an entire board if the directors resisted the strategic redirection that most investors advocated. When directors of Darden Restaurants (the largest operator of full-service restaurants in the United States) decided on a spin-off that many investors had opposed, Starboard Value LP—with the support of unhappy institutional investors—ousted them all.[3]

Strengthening a board's capacity for thinking and acting strategically calls for more carefully considering who comes onto the board, who remains on the board, and above all how the board is organized and led as an active partner with management. When individual directors are not adding strategic and leadership value, equity investors often press incumbent directors to recruit directors who will, and once on board, new directors should explain "how you bring value to investors," argues Vanguard Group chief executive William McNabb.[4]

Activist investors, with the backing of institutional investors, have also targeted company leadership. Here the outside focus is on the failure of the top management team either to embrace a high-value strategy or to execute it well. Activist investors in effect press companies to do what DuPont had forced itself to do in 2015.

In 2012, an activist investor forced changes on Yahoo Inc., the technology firm whose services include internet search, instant messaging, digital media, and online advertising. At the time, Yahoo employed 11,700, booked annual revenue of $5 billion, and held a market capitalization near $18 billion.[5]

Daniel Loeb, manager of the Third Point LLC hedge fund that had amassed a 6% stake (about $1 billion) in Yahoo's stock, had been critical of the company's declining fortunes and frequent executive turnover. The board had appointed six CEOs over 11 years. To remedy matters, Loeb proposed a slate of four dissident directors to implement a strategic redirection that he had already been advocating, including greater focus on the firm's media and advertising business. In May 2012, Yahoo agreed to bring three of Third Point's director nominees onto its board, and two months later the board recruited a new management team.[6]

These developments are a sharp reminder that, as we said at the outset of the book, investors are placing greater pressure on company directors to exercise more strategic leadership of their firm. Directors, in turn, are increasingly pressing their executives to more effectively integrate application of their strategy and leadership, and executives are insisting on the same from their managerial ranks. Though in our view the strategic leader's roadmap should be embraced by all managers if they are to optimize their working impact on the company, investors and directors are increasingly demanding it in any case.

Conclusion
Becoming a Strategic Leader

C ompany strategy and its leadership are inextricably joined at the hip. One without the other can take a firm toward the abyss, as we have seen at Uber, or together they can grow the firm globally, as we have witnessed at Lenovo. Box C.1 provides six foundations for thinking strategically and leading actively at the same time.

The Roadmap in Action

As we leave you to strengthen your own strategic leader's roadmap, we conclude with a moment from the business world that helps makes a final point: All of the strategic and leadership actions referenced here can be strengthened along the way. None are innate, and your personal roadmap can be bolstered by pushing yourself toward greater mastery, recruiting mentors who facilitate mastery, and learning from experience to round out mastery. To anchor this, we return to ITT's Denise Ramos.

Ramos had studied economics at Purdue, then business at the University of Chicago, completing her MBA at age 22 with a major in finance. "I always enjoyed numbers and how they related to the operations of the business," she recalled, and "that really informed how I thought." Her first job out of school was a good match for her early credentials, and a good place for executive development. At Atlantic Richfield Co., a prominent energy supplier, she joined a

Box C.1. The Strategic Leader's Roadmap

1. **Learn to lead strategically.** Draw on directed learning, personal coaching, and instructive experience to build a capacity to lead strategically as it applies to both oneself and those in lower layers. *Example*: Executives at Cisco and GlaxoSmithKline used these three avenues of learning to identify and build leadership in themselves and their ranks.

2. **Focus on product differentiation, relative cost, superior value proposition, and sustained value proposition.** In posing questions on strategy and leadership in each of these four areas, consider how the enterprise is best positioned in its markets and then whether the right people and architecture are in place to achieve the strategy. *Example*: Larry Culp led Danaher, Steve Jobs led Apple, and Indra Nooyi led PepsiCo to adopt a more sustainable value proposition.

3. **Ensure strategic fit, convey strategic intent, layer leadership, and decide deliberatively.** Apply them as a bundle to integrate company strategy and its leadership. *Example*: Chile's president Sebastián Piñera used them to lead his country's comeback from a natural disaster, as did US president Ronald Reagan in pressing for the Soviet Union's dissolution.

4. **Lead executable initiatives driven by your value proposition, specific initiatives, and operational leaders.** Actively transform strategic thinking into operational reality. *Example*: Cisco's John Chambers acquired and invested in new technologies to provide customers with end-to-end solutions for their emergent technology needs.

5. **Build boards that provide strategic leadership.** Well-designed and well-composed, governing boards can serve as strategic partners of management. *Example*: Executives at Lenovo drew on the business experience and expertise of their directors for succeeding in the international market in personal computers and related technologies.

6. **Develop managers who can think and act strategically.** Recruit and build managers who think and act strategically

within their own tier. *Example*: As we will explain, ITT Inc. CEO Denise Ramos developed her strategic leadership through learning, mentoring, and experience.

---

finance team built by a CFO who believed that its work should be of direct value to both the corporate and divisional levels. As a result, he rotated its members, including Ramos, every other year among accounting, treasury, and other finance functions to strengthen their understanding of the whole enterprise.[1]

Later, Ramos joined the finance function of Yum! Brands Inc., home of KFC, Pizza Hut, and Taco Bell, where she worked to further broaden her horizons. "I really wanted to challenge myself to see what I could do that was both different and interesting," she said. Later, when she became the first chief executive of the newly created ITT Inc., Ramos was not sure she had the complete skill set necessary. She had fast-tracked up to the C-suite of prebreakup ITT, but she had never carried direct profit and loss responsibility for an operation. But the spin-off governing board chair, Frank MacInnis, had deemed Ramos already well prepared. He had been impressed when she had reported as CFO to the old ITT board, on which MacInnis had served. "I realized," he said, "it was the kind of report that one would expect from a CEO," meaning that, while she did not yet have to make the final calls, she grasped their complexity. "She was CEO," MacInnis summed up, "before she was *the* CEO."

MacInnis, who had been on the ITT board for a decade before the company split, and who had served for sixteen years as chief executive of EMCOR Group, a Fortune 500 engineering and construction company, placed himself at Ramos's side as needed to help fill the gaps in her experience or skill set. She appreciated she had little direct familiarity with how to run manufacturing lines or market industrial products. "I knew this was my weak spot," she said, but she vowed to learn what she still needed from her engineering and marketing subordinates.

We close our account with a focus on the integrated value of strategy and leadership in one of the most celebrated moments in the sport of mountaineering: the first summiting of Mount Everest. It is a story of strategy, leadership, and their dual application, and without both working together, the world's highest summit at 29,032 feet would likely not have been reached by that British expedition on May 29, 1953.[2]

The British had been attempting to climb Mount Everest since 1921. Two mountaineers on the second expedition in 1924, George Mallory and Andrew Irvine, had disappeared near the top, and five subsequent tries had also fallen short. And now the competition was closing in. Although Mount Everest had been named in the West after an English surveyor, a Swiss expedition had nearly reached its summit in 1952, and French and German expeditions were preparing to try next.

The British Himalayan Committee had decided to attack the mountain from the southern, Nepalese side, where a narrow cleavage appeared to offer a feasible route to the top in a way that the traditional northern side in Tibet had not. To lead this latest attempt, the committee appointed John Hunt as expedition leader, a little-known career military officer based in India who specialized in logistics and who was to apply a new strategy for reaching the Himalayan summit, soon to become standard in high-altitude mountaineering. It called for an army of climbers, porters, Sherpas, and yaks that would move methodically up the mountain, shuttling supplies and climbers to ever-higher camps. The goal was to put two climbers at a high camp near the summit, and Hunt's strategy was to move a pair with supplies up a pyramid of people to that site.

Consistent with the logistics-focused strategy, John Hunt placed a supply cache high on the summit ridge, and late on May 28, 1953, Edmund Hillary and Tenzing Norgay reached the cache to hunker down for the night. At 4 a.m. on May 29, they arose for the final ascent, and at 11:30 a.m. Hillary snapped the photo: Norgay, ice ax raised aloft in victory, left foot planted atop the highest point on Earth. It was an extraordinary moment that rightly made Hillary and Norgay legends. Their positioning to reach the summit had come from an expedition leader who had embraced and effectively executed a logistics-driven strategy to place them at the high camp.

Strategic leadership is vital for reaching most summits, whether in mountaineering, politics, or business, and the challenge is thus to build it well before it is needed on summit day. And for that, becoming a strategic leader oneself and developing strategic leadership in others is one of the great callings of our era.

It is vital for managers to treat strategy and leadership as an integrated package, ensuring they fit together and are acquired and exercised jointly. This is especially true in an era marked by uncertainty, complexity, and change, where company strategy and leadership are especially consequential for a firm's performance. And though we sometimes say an individual is a gifted strategist or a natural-born leader, we know from research and experience that both are learned—and that we can all become more strategic leaders if we stay on the right path. Self-directed study, personal coaching, and stretch experience provide the proven avenue for getting there.

References

Adelman, Kenneth. *Reagan at Reykjavik: Forty-Eight Hours That Ended the Cold War.* New York: Broadside Books/HarperCollins, 2014.

Anand, Bharat, David J. Collis, and Sophie Hood. Case, "Danaher Corporation" Boston: Harvard Business School, 2015.

Andrade, Gregor, Mark Mitchell, and Eric Stafford. "New Evidence and Perspectives on Mergers." *Journal of Economic Perspectives* 15 (2001): 103–120.

Aon Hewitt. "Top Companies for Leaders." 2015. https://www.aonhumancapital.ae /getattachment/d2dab903-db68-461a-9c4d-91dbe7cb3837/file.aspx?disposition =attachment.

Baird Equity Research. *ITT Inc.*, report, August 2, 2018.

Baker, Gerald. "PepsiCo's Indra Nooyi on the Tricky Path from CFO to CEO." *Wall Street Journal*, June 24, 2014.

Benoit, David. "Dow, DuPont Deal Cements Activists' Rise." *Wall Street Journal*, December 11, 2015.

Bossidy, Larry, and Ram Charan. *Execution: The Disciplines of Getting Things Done.* New York: Crown Business, 2002.

Cappelli, Peter, Harbir Singh, Jitendra Singh, and Michael Useem. *The India Way: How India's Top Business Leaders Are Revolutionizing Management.* Boston: Harvard Business Press, 2010.

Carey, Dennis, Dan Phelan, and Michael Useem. "Picking the Right Insider for CEO Succession." *Harvard Business Review*, January 2009.

Chambers, John. "In a Near-Death Event, a Corporate Rite of Passage," Corner Office, *New York Times*, August 1, 2009. https://www.nytimes.com/2009/08/02 /business/02corner.html.

Chambers, John. "Cisco's CEO on Staying Ahead of Technology Shifts." *Harvard Business Review*, May 2015.

Chambers, John. *Connecting the Dots: Lessons for Leadership in a Startup World.* New York: Hachette Books, 2018.

Charan, Ram, Dennis Carey, and Michael Useem. *Boards That Lead.* Boston: Harvard Business Review Press, 2014.

Charan, Ram, Michael Useem, and Dennis Carey. "Your Board Should Think Like Activists." *HBR Blog Network*, February 9, 2015. https://hbr.org/2015/02/your-board -should-be-full-of-activists.

Davis, Gerald F. *Managed by the Markets: How Finance Re-shaped America*. New York: Oxford University Press, 2009.

Dempsey, Martin E. "Mission Command White Paper." Chairman of the US Joint Chiefs of Staff, 2012.

Dranove, David, and Sonia Marciano. *Kellogg on Strategy: Concepts, Tools, and Frameworks for Practitioners*. Hoboken, NJ: Wiley, 2005.

Efrati, Amir, and Joann S. Lublin. "Thompson Resigns as CEO of Yahoo." *Wall Street Journal*, May 13, 2012a.

Efrati, Amir, and Joann S. Lublin. "Yahoo CEO's Downfall." *Wall Street Journal*, May 15, 2012b.

Fligstein, Neil. *The Transformation of Corporate Capital*. Boston: Harvard University Press, 1990.

Freda, Fabrizio. Lecture at the Wharton School, Philadelphia, Pennsylvania, February 25, 2015.

Fryer, Bronwyn, and Thomas A. Stewart. "Cisco Sees the Future." *Harvard Business Review*, November 2008.

General Electric Crotonville. "The Future of Leadership." 2016. https://www.ge.com /sites/default/files/GE_Crotonville_Future_of_Leadership.pdf.

Hamel, Gary, and C. K. Prahalad. "Strategic Intent." *Harvard Business Review*, June 2010 (first published May 1989).

Harvard Business Review. *Strategy: Create and Implement the Best Strategy for Your Success*. Harvard Business Essentials Series. Boston: Harvard Business Press, 2005.

Harvard Business Review. *Executing Strategy*. Pocket Mentor Series. Boston: Harvard Business Press, 2009.

Harvard Business Review. *Thinking Strategically*. Pocket Mentor Series. Boston: Harvard Business Press, 2010.

Haskett, Gordon. Research Advisor, *ITT*, report, October 12, 2018.

Hitt, Michael A., Katalin Takacs Haynes, and Roy Serpa. "Strategic Leadership for the 21st Century." *Business Horizons* 53 (2010): 437–444.

Holstein, William J. "Lenovo Goes Global." *Strategy + Business* 76 (Autumn 2014). https://www.strategy-business.com/article/00274.

Hrebiniak, Lawrence G. *Making Strategy Work: Leading Effective Execution and Change*. Upper Saddle, NJ: Pearson Education, 2005.

IKEA. "IKEA Vision, Culture and Values." 2021. https://ikea.jobs.cz/en/vision -culture-and-values/#:~:text='To%20create%20a%20better%20everyday,be%20 able%20to%20afford%20them'.

Isaac, Mike. "Uber Founder Travis Kalanick Resigns as C.E.O.," *New York Times*, June 21, 2017. https://www.nytimes.com/2017/06/21/technology/uber-ceo-travis-kalanick.html.

Isaacson, Walter. *Steve Jobs*. New York: Simon and Schuster, 2011.

Jargon, Julie, and David Benoit. "How a Shareholder Coup at Olive Garden's Owner Sparked a Turnaround." *Wall Street Journal*, April 5, 2016.

Jenkins, Aric. "Meet the CEO of the Insurance Company Growing Faster Than Apple." *Fortune*, November 15, 2018. https://fortune.com/2018/11/15/progressive-insurance-ceo-tricia-griffith.

Kahneman, Daniel. *Thinking, Fast and Slow*. New York: Farrar, Straus and Giroux, 2011.

Kaiser, Kevin, Michael Pich, and I. J. Schecter. *Becoming a Top Manager: Tools and Lessons in Transitioning to General Management*. Hoboken, NJ: Jossey-Bass, 2015.

King, Ian. "Andy Grove, Who Taught Silicon Valley How to Do Business, Dies." *Bloomberg Technology*, March 21, 2016. http://www.bloomberg.com/news/articles/2016-03-22/andy-grove-the-man-who-taught-silicon-valley-how-to-do-business.

Kluger, Jeffrey, and James Lovell. *Lost Moon: The Perilous Voyage of Apollo 13*. New York: Houghton Mifflin, 1994.

Kocienda, Ken. *Creative Selection: Inside Apple's Design Process during the Golden Age of Steve Jobs*. New York: St. Martin's Press, 2018.

Kranz, Eugene. *Failure Is Not an Option: Mission Control from Mercury to Apollo 13 and Beyond*. New York: Simon & Schuster, 2009.

Krupp, Steven, and Paul J. H. Schoemaker. *Winning the Long Game: How Strategic Leaders Shape the Future*. New York: PublicAffairs Press, 2014.

Lafley, A. G., and Roger L. Martin. *Playing to Win: How Strategy Really Works*. Boston: Harvard Business Review Press, 2013.

Liang, Neng, and Michael Useem. Case, "Lenovo 2009: The Role of Board Chairman in a Turnaround." China Europe International Business School, 2014.

Ling, Zhijun. *The Lenovo Affair: The Growth of China's Computer Giant and Its Takeover of IBM-PC*. Translated by Martha Avery. Hoboken, NJ: Wiley, 2006.

Loeb, Daniel S. "Letter to the Yahoo Inc. Board of Directors." Third Point LLC, September 8, 2011. https://www.sec.gov/Archives/edgar/data/1011006/000089914011000474/a6970038b.htm.

Lohr, Steve. "I.B.M. Sought at China Partnership, Not Just a Sale." *New York Times*, December 13, 2004.

Lorsch, Jay W., and Elizabeth MacIver. *Pawns or Potentates: The Reality of America's Corporate Boards*. Boston: Harvard Business School Press, 1989.

Macrotrends. "Procter & Gamble: Number of Employees 2006–2021." 2021. https://www.macrotrends.net/stocks/charts/PG/procter-gamble/number-of-employees.

McKinsey & Company. "McKinsey Conversations with Global Leaders: John Chambers of Cisco." *McKinsey Quarterly*, July 2009. http://www.mckinsey.com /industries/high-tech/our-insights/mckinsey-conversations-with-global-leaders-john -chambers-of-cisco.

McNabb, F. William, III. "Getting to Know You: Sharing Practical Governance Viewpoints." Lecture at John Weinberg Center for Corporate Governance, University of Delaware, October 30, 2014.

Merced, Michael J. de la, and Evelyn M. Rusli. "Yahoo's Chief to Leave as Company Strikes Deal with Loeb." *New York Times*, May 13, 2012.

Montgomery, Cynthia. *The Strategist: Be the Leader Your Business Needs*. New York: Harper Business, 2012.

Narayan, Adi, and Prabhudatta Mishra. "India Asks PepsiCo to Help Make School Lunches Healthier." *Bloomberg Business*, August 27, 2014.

Olson, Aaron K., and B. Keith Simerson. *Leading with Strategic Thinking*. Hoboken, NJ: Wiley, 2015.

Porter, Michael. "What Is Strategy?" *Harvard Business Review*, November–December 1996.

Puranam, Phasnish, Harbir Singh, and Saikat Chaudhuri. "Integrating Acquired Capabilities: When Structural Integration Is (Un)necessary." *Organization Science* 20 (2009): 313–328.

Qiao, Gina, and Yolanda Conyers. *The Lenovo Way: Managing a Diverse Global Company for Optimal Performance*. New York: McGraw-Hill, 2014.

Reingold, Jennifer. "PepsiCo's CEO Was Right. Now What?" *Fortune*, June 5, 2015.

Rusli, Evelyn M. "Activist Investor Charts Plan to Revitalize Yahoo." *New York Times*, March 8, 2012.

S&P Dow Jones Indices LLC. "S&P 500 2014: Global Sales." 2016. http://us.spindices .com/documents/research/research-sp-500-2014-global-sales.pdf.

Seabrook, John. "Snacks for a Fat Planet: PepsiCo Takes Stock of the Obesity Epidemic." *New Yorker*, May 16, 2011. http://www.newyorker.com/magazine/2011/05 /16/snacks-for-a-fat-planet.

Sidhu, Inder. *Doing Both: Capturing Today's Profit and Driving Tomorrow's Growth*. Upper Saddle River, NJ: FT Press, 2010.

Singh, Harbir, Saikat Chaudhuri, and Rachel Shelton. "Cisco's Acquisition Strategy (1993 to 2000): Value Growth Through Buying Early-Stage Companies." Wharton School, University of Pennsylvania, 2008a.

Singh, Harbir, Saikat Chaudhuri, and Rachel Shelton. "Cisco's Acquisition Strategy (2001 to 2008): Adapting to Changing Market Conditions." Wharton School, University of Pennsylvania, 2008b.

Smith, Aaron. "Ikea Lifting Minimum Wage to Nearly $11 per Hour." *CNN Money*, June 26, 2014. http://money.cnn.com/2014/06/26/news/companies/ikea-minimum-wage/.

Solomon, Steven Davidoff. "In DuPont Fight, Activist Investor Picks a Strong Target." *New York Times*, January 27, 2015.

Sorkin, Andrew Ross, and Evelyn M. Rusli. "A Yahoo Search Calls Up a Chief from Google." *New York Times*, July 16, 2012.

Statista. "Worldwide Revenue of Pfizer's Lipitor from 2003 to 2019." 2021. www .statista.com/statistics/254341/pfizers-worldwide-viagra-revenues-since-2003/#:~:text =During%202019%2C%20Pfizer's%20Lipitor%20generated,billion%20U.S.%20 dollars%20in%202006.

Tedlow, Richard S. "The Education of Andy Grove." *Fortune*, December 12, 2005.

Tedlow, Richard S. *Andy Grove: The Life and Times of an American*. New York: Portfolio, 2006.

Third Point LLC. Schedule 13 D. Securities and Exchange Commission. February 14, 2012.

Tichy, Noel. *The Leadership Engine*. New York: Harper Business, 2002.

Trahan, François, and Katherine Krantz. *The Era of Uncertainty: Global Investment Strategies, Inflation, Deflation, and the Middle Ground*. Hoboken, NJ: Wiley, 2011.

US Army. "Army Doctrine Publication 6-0: Mission Command." 2012.

Useem, Michael. *Investor Capitalism: How Money Managers Are Changing the Face of Corporate America*. New York: Basic Books, 1996.

Useem, Michael. "Corporate Leadership in a Globalizing Equity Market." *Academy of Management Executive* 12 (1998): 43–59.

Useem, Michael. "Indra Nooyi: New Ideas for This Pepsi Generation." *U.S. News & World Report* 145, no. 12 (December 2008): 49.

Useem, Michael. "John Chambers: Whether Up or Down, Always Innovating." *U.S. News & World Report* 146, no. 10 (November 2009): 54.

Useem, Michael. *The Edge: How 10 CEOs Learned to Lead—and the Lessons for Us All*. New York: PublicAffairs Books, 2021.

Useem, Michael, and Dennis Carey. "WorldCom, Inc.: Recruiting a New Chief Executive in 2002." Wharton School, University of Pennsylvania, 2008.

Useem, Michael, Rodrigo Jordán, and Matko Koljatic. "How to Lead During a Crisis: Lessons from the Rescue of the Chilean Miners." *MIT Sloan Management Review* 53 (Fall 2011): 1–7.

Useem, Michael, Howard Kunreuther, and Erwann Michel-Kerjan. *Leadership Dispatches: Chile's Extraordinary Comeback from Disaster*. Redwood City, CA: Stanford University Press, 2015.

Useem, Michael, and Neng Liang. "Globalizing the Company Board: Lessons from China's Lenovo." In *Boardroom Realities: Building Leaders Across Your Board*, edited by Jay A. Conger, 401–444. San Francisco, CA: Jossey-Bass, 2009.

Useem, Michael, Neng Liang, and Rachel Shelton. "Lenovo's Decision to Acquire IBM's PC Division in 2004: The Evolution of a New Approach to Governance." Wharton School and China Europe International Business School, 2008.

Useem, Michael, Harbir Singh, Neng Liang, and Peter Cappelli. *Fortune Makers: The Leaders Creating China's Great Global Companies.* New York: PublicAffairs Press, 2017.

Useem, Michael, and Jerry Useem. "The Board That Conquered Everest." *Fortune*, October 27, 2003.

Walker, Gordon. *Modern Competitive Strategy.* New York: McGraw Hill Higher Education, 2015.

Weber, Elke U., and Eric J. Johnson. "Decisions Under Uncertainty: Psychological, Economic, and Neuroeconomic Explanations of Risk Preference." In *Neuroeconomics: Decision Making and the Brain*, edited by Paul Glimcher, Colin Camerer, Ernst Fehr, and Russell Poldrack, 127–144. New York: Elsevier Science, 2008.

Womack, James P., Daniel T. Jones, and Daniel Roos, *The Machine That Changed the World.* New York: Scribner, 1990.

Yoffie, David B., and Michael A. Cusumano. *Strategy Rules: Five Timeless Lessons from Bill Gates, Andy Grove, and Steve Jobs.* New York: Harper Business, 2015.

Notes

Introduction

1 Isaacson, 2011.

2 Isaac, 2017.

3 This section draws on Useem, 2021.

4 Jenkins, 2018.

5 S&P Dow Jones Indices, 2016; Trahan and Krantz, 2011.

6 See, for instance, Cappelli, Singh, Singh, and Useem, 2010.

7 Tedlow, 2005, 2006. We draw on the following partial list of personal interviews that one or both of us conducted, in some cases in collaboration with other colleagues:

Individual	Position	Company	Date of Interview
William Amelio	Chief executive officer	Lenovo	August 13, 2007; January 31, 2009; July 14, 2009
Edward Breen	Chief executive officer	Tyco International and DuPont	2015–2019
Gregory Q. Brown	Chief executive officer	Motorola Solutions	December 19, 2013
John Chambers	Chief executive officer	Cisco Systems	August 27, 2009; November 26, 2018
Fabrizio Freda	Chief executive officer	Estée Lauder Companies	2014–2019
Jean-Pierre Garnier	Chief executive officer	GlaxoSmithKline	2007–2008
Laurence Golborne	Minister of mines	Republic of Chile	2013–2014
Raj Gupta	Chief executive officer	Rohm & Haas	2015–2019
He Zhiqiang	Chief technology officer	Lenovo	2008

(continued)

Individual	Position	Company	Date of Interview
Bo Ilsoe	Partner	Nokia Growth Partners	2018–2019
Christian Tang-Jespersen	Chief executive officer	Heptagon Micro Optics	2018–2019
Chanda Kochhar	Chief executive officer	ICICI Bank	September 17, 2015
Liu Chuanzhi	Executive chair	Lenovo	2004, 2008, 2013
Jack Ma	Founder and executive chair	Alibaba Group	February 13, 2013
Indra Nooyi	Chief executive officer	PepsiCo	April 11, 2019
Sebastián Piñera	President	Republic of Chile	2013–2015
Denise Ramos	Chief executive officer	ITT Inc.	2018–2019
Steven Reinemund	Former chief executive officer	PepsiCo	January 20, 2009
Glenn Tilton	Former chief executive officer	Texaco and United Airlines	January 22, 2015
Shan Weijian	Nonexecutive director	Lenovo	2008
Yang Yuanqing	Chief executive officer	Lenovo	2008

Chapter 1

1 IKEA, 2021.

2 Smith, 2014.

3 See, for instance, Dranove and Marciano, 2005; *Harvard Business Review*, 2005, 2009, 2010; Hitt, Haynes, and Serpa, 2010; Hrebiniak, 2005; Kaiser, Pich, and Schecter, 2015; Krupp and Schoemaker, 2014; Montgomery, 2012; Olson and Simerson, 2015.

4 Macrotrends, 2021.

5 Lafley and Martin, 2013.

6 Statista, 2021.

7 Michael Porter, 1996, first proposed a characterization of competitive position by placing relative cost on the horizontal axis and "non-price buyer value" on the vertical axis. Our adaptation is to reference "differentiation" as a driver of willingness to pay premium prices as the vertical axis while retaining relative cost on the horizontal axis. Differentiation is close in spirit to non-price buyer

value but more explicitly tied to willingness of customers to pay. Walker, 2015, uses a similar plot with differentiation and production cost as axes to define competitive positioning.

8 Singh, Chaudhuri, and Shelton, 2008a, 2008b; McKinsey & Company, 2009.

9 Chambers, 2018.

10 This section draws on Useem, 2021.

11 Fryer and Stewart, 2008; Sidhu, 2010; Useem, 2009.

12 Fryer and Stewart, 2008.

13 This section draws on Useem, 2021.

14 Haskett, 2018 ("we believe"); Baird Equity Research, 2018 ("healthy position").

Chapter 2

1 Freda, 2015.

Chapter 3

1 Aon Hewitt, 2015.

2 Tichy, 2002.

3 General Electric Crotonville, 2016.

4 King, 2016.

5 Baker, 2014.

6 Chambers, 2015, 2018.

7 Interview with John Chambers for Useem, 2009.

8 Useem, 2009; see also Chambers, 2015, and Fryer and Stewart, 2008.

9 Tedlow, 2005; see also Tedlow, 2006.

Chapter 4

1 Fligstein, 1990.

2 Carey, Phelan, and Useem, 2009, 1.

3 Useem and Carey, 2008; Charan, Carey, and Useem, 2014.

Chapter 5

1 Hamel and Prahalad, 2010.

2 US Army, 2012; Dempsey, 2012.

3 US Army, 2012; Dempsey, 2012.

4 Useem, Kunreuther, and Michel-Kerjan, 2015.

5 Adelman, 2014.

Chapter 6

1   Kluger and Lovell, 1994; Kranz, 2009.

2   Useem, Jordán, and Koljatic, 2011.

3   Isaacson, 2011.

4   Kocienda, 2018.

5   Kocienda, 2018.

6   Kocienda, 2018.

7   Kocienda, 2018.

Chapter 7

1   Weber and Johnson, 2008; Kahneman, 2011.

2   Kahneman, 2011.

3   Yoffie and Cusumano, 2015.

Chapter 8

1   Bossidy and Charan, 2002, 6.

2   Womack, Jones, and Roos, 1990.

3   Anand, Collis, Hood, 2015.

Chapter 9

1   This section draws on Narayan and Mishra, 2014; Seabrook, 2011.

2   Useem, 2008.

3   Reingold, 2015; Useem, 2008.

4   The account of Jack Ma and Alibaba is drawn from Useem, Singh, Liang, and Cappelli, 2017.

Chapter 10

1   Andrade, Mitchell, and Stafford, 2001; Puranam, Singh, and Chaudhuri, 2009.

Chapter 11

1   Lorsch and MacIver, 1989.

2   Davis, 2009; Useem, 1996, 1998.

3   Charan, Carey, and Useem, 2014; Cappelli, Singh, Singh, and Useem, 2010; Useem, Singh, Liang, and Cappelli, 2017.

4   This section draws on Holstein, 2014; Liang and Useem, 2014; Ling, 2006; Lohr, 2004; Qiao and Conyers, 2014; Useem, Liang, and Shelton, 2008; and Useem, Singh, Liang, and Cappelli, 2017.

5 Useem and Liang, 2009.

6 Useem and Liang, 2009.

Chapter 12

1 Solomon, 2015.

2 Benoit, 2015.

3 Jargon and Benoit, 2016; Charan, Useem, and Carey, 2015.

4 McNabb, 2014.

5 Rusli, 2012.

6 Efrati and Lublin, 2012a, 2012b; Loeb, 2011; Merced and Rusli, 2012; Sorkin and Rusli, 2012; Third Point LLC, 2012.

Conclusion

1 This section draws on Useem, 2021.

2 This section draws on Useem and Useem, 2003.

Index

Page numbers in italics refer to boxes and figures.

About the Authors

Harbir Singh is Mack Professor of Management, codirector of the Mack Institute for Innovation Management, and faculty director of the Huntsman Program, Wharton School, University of Pennsylvania. His research and teaching interests include corporate governance, corporate restructuring, joint ventures, management buyouts, and strategies for corporate acquisitions.

Michael Useem is Professor of Management and faculty director of the McNulty Leadership Program and the Center for Leadership and Change Management, Wharton School, University of Pennsylvania. His research and teaching interests include corporate governance, risk management, decision making, organizational leadership, and change management.

About Wharton School Press

Wharton School Press, the book publishing arm of the Wharton School of the University of Pennsylvania, was established to inspire bold, insightful thinking within the global business community.

Wharton School Press publishes a select list of award-winning, best-selling, and thought-leading books that offer trusted business knowledge to help leaders at all levels meet the challenges of today and the opportunities of tomorrow. Led by a spirit of innovation and experimentation, Wharton School Press leverages ground-breaking digital technologies and has pioneered a fast-reading business book format that fits readers' busy lives, allowing them to swiftly emerge with the tools and information needed to make an impact. Wharton School Press books offer guidance and inspiration on a variety of topics, including leadership, management, strategy, innovation, entrepreneurship, finance, marketing, social impact, public policy, and more.

Wharton School Press also operates an online bookstore featuring a curated selection of influential books by Wharton School faculty and Press authors published by a wide range of leading publishers.

To find books that will inspire and empower you to increase your impact and expand your personal and professional horizons, visit *wsp.wharton.upenn.edu*.

UNIVERSITY *of* PENNSYLVANIA

About the Wharton School

Founded in 1881 as the world's first collegiate business school, the Wharton School of the University of Pennsylvania is shaping the future of business by incubating ideas, driving insights, and creating leaders who change the world. With a faculty of more than 235 renowned professors, Wharton has 5,000 undergraduate, MBA, executive MBA, and doctoral students. Each year 13,000 professionals from around the world advance their careers through Wharton Executive Education's individual, company-customized, and online programs. More than 100,000 Wharton alumni form a powerful global network of leaders who transform business every day. For more information, visit *www.wharton.upenn.edu.*

Lightning Source UK Ltd.
Milton Keynes UK
UKHW010056160921
390665UK00001B/20

9 781613 631522